VOLUME 2

I AM A
creator.

15 true stories *of* remarkable people earning a living doing work they love.

MADE BY CONVERTKIT

ISBN 978-1-7356767-0-8

Book design and layout by Taylor Roy
Written by Isa Adney
Editing by Dani Stewart and Amanda Johnson
Production coordination by Tania Tercero

Printed and bound in the USA

Published by ConvertKit
PO Box 761
Boise, ID 83701

Visit convertkit.com

This book is dedicated to all the creators out there who create even in the midst of hardship, chaos, injustice, or tragedy—changing lives along the way.

Contents

---

by Barrett Brooks,
COO of ConvertKit

It's May 3, 2019. I'm standing at ConvertKit's booth at the Everything Food Conference in a conference center outside of Salt Lake City, Utah.

It's the last networking session of the day. I'm tired, but I think I can power through.

Several hundred creators are walking around the sponsor ballroom, visiting booths to fill in their sponsor bingo cards. In between stamping bingo cards and showing a potential customer our software, two women walk up and wait patiently in line. One of them picks up one of our coffee table books, *I Am A Blogger.*

I say hello, introduce myself, and ask, "How can I help?" One of them asks, "Who wrote this book?"

I dive into the story of why we made the book and how we traveled around the country to conduct the interviews. Finally, I share that I did the interviews and wrote the introduction, but that it was a team effort to design, write, edit, and print the book.

"Oh, *YOU* wrote the introduction?" one woman says.

Uh oh...

"Yes?"

"Tanya here loves this book. Tell him the story, Tanya," her friend says.

"One afternoon, my daughter's tutor came over to the house," Tanya explains. "When she arrived, she handed me a copy of this book. She told me her husband had an extra copy and it made her think of me, so she brought it as a gift."

She goes on, "I was a lawyer at the time and had been working on my food blog for a while. It had started to earn some money, but I wasn't sure if I should go full-time. It felt irresponsible and everyone around me thought I was crazy."

"Then I read the introduction," she says as she opens the book and reads the last paragraph of my own words back to me.

We hope you enjoy reading these 16 stories as much as we've enjoyed telling them. But more than anything, we hope when you close the back cover of this book you walk away with one very clear message: you are every bit as capable, worthy, and ready to take the leap as the people in this book.

Will you?

"In that moment, I knew it was time to quit my job," Tanya tells me. "I took a photo of it and sent it to a friend along with 'I'm quitting my job.' And I did. I just went full-time on my blog. This is my first event as a full-time blogger. This book made it feel normal to earn a living like this," she says as she looks up with a smile on her face.

"Thank you for making it," she shares.

"Wow. Thank you for sharing that with me," I respond. "Would you like another copy to take with you?"

Tanya walked away with another book in hand, making her way through the sponsor ballroom and through her journey as a creator.

What I didn't tell her is that her story gave me chills. It made me tear up.

Yes, we're in the business of helping creators earn a living. Everything we do is for that purpose alone. But we're creators ourselves too.

When you set out to chase a wild idea like making a series of documentary short films and a coffee table book about earning a living as a creator, you sometimes get responses like "Wait, what? Why would you do that?" It's very similar to what you might hear when you tell your friends you're quitting your job to grow your food blog.

"We're building an iconic brand. We want to make creators the hero of our story as a company," I'd say. This is true, but the thing I would rarely say out loud is that we were doing it because we hoped it would change someone's life.

When a person you've never met walks up to you at a conference in

Layton, Utah, and says your words in a coffee table book changed her life, well, it's enough to give you the chills.

Changing people's lives—that is the spirit of being a creator.

It sounds trite. Corny. Altruistic.

Creators know it doesn't matter how it sounds because their email inboxes and Instagram DMs are filled with stories just like this one. Readers, listeners, viewers, and fans write to tell you how you've changed their lives.

Creators are in the business of changing lives. It's why we wake up and make art, even when it's terrifying. Because nothing is more empowering than taking control of our own lives and building the future.

The future belongs to creators. And as creators we get a say in what the world will look like.

Creators are change-makers. Artists. Chefs. Athletes. Fashion designers. Activists. Photographers. Storytellers.

Creators come from all backgrounds, countries, ethnicities, genders, sexual orientations, shapes, sizes, and abilities.

They are the heart of our culture. They lead us, teach us, entertain us, and inspire us—giving us hope when hope is hard to come by. And in times like these, we all need something to hope for.

As you read the stories in this book—the second coffee table book from the team at ConvertKit and the first under the new name of *I Am A*

Creator—I hope you see yourself in these pages.

Just like the words that inspired Tanya to take the leap, I'll close with a call to action: When you close this book, I hope you know that you are a creator. In fact, we're all creators. Some of us just haven't gotten started yet.

The only difference between the people in these stories and you: a couple years of work dedicated to an idea you care deeply about. You're capable. You just have to start.

Will you?

Tanya Harris, food blogger

INTRODUCTION

by Isa Adney,
Storyteller at ConvertKit

I'll never forget walking into Tanya Harris' calm kitchen, sitting in Dave Barnes' bright studio, or walking along the freezing Florence, Oregon, coast in the rain with Jessica Bird.

The creators in this book changed me.

I found treasure in every story.

Jessica showed me what it really looks like to savor each moment—even the cold and rainy ones. Courtland showed me that big, crazy dreams can come true even when you least expect it, and Jenell showed me what it looks like to shine brightly in an unjust world.

I loved looking into their eyes, touring their creative spaces, and listening to their life stories.

And now it's your turn.

In these stories you'll find luck, magic, and those oh-my-gosh-I-can't-believe-that-happened moments.

You'll also find heartache, tragedy, failure, rejection, imposter syndrome, and fear, fear, fear.

We want to share what it's really like to be a creator.

We want to show you what keeps creators going when things get tough.

Because we're creators too. And we know how hard it is on those doubt-filled days when you wonder if you are good enough or if your art is good enough or if you really have what it takes.

The best and scariest part about being a creator is that there aren't a lot of rules.

That's why we like stories.

In these stories, we hope you find strength for your road ahead as well as delightful moments (like the pictures of Deborah's goats), inspiring ideas (like how Glo deals with imposter syndrome), and reminders that it's never too late to start a new dream (like Steve and Azul).

But there is one story that rises above the rest—the most important, beautiful, and special story here— the one this book is really all about.

The story of the creator holding this book.

As you turn each page, we hope you remember that your story is just as magical, just as beautiful, just as inspiring, and just as incredibly precious—because it's yours.

Keep going. Keep creating.

CHAPTER ONE

Knowing your worth

SELF-DOUBT IS NORMAL.

Every creator experiences it again and again (and again).

And don't worry: we're not going to tell you that you always have to believe in yourself.

You don't.

But you do have to *sometimes* believe in yourself.

Just a little. Just enough to take one tiny step. Then another, then another.

The bravest creators take those steps even when they don't feel like they believe in themselves. They move forward anyway because they are just *kind of* curious (a form of belief they may not recognize as such).

The creators in this chapter began their journeys with small steps and tiny sparks: answering a question, following an idea, exploring a dream, or creating something they hoped would help someone else.

They didn't always know their worth. But by creating anyway, it somehow almost always revealed itself.

The natural, inherent value of you

What happens when you ask yourself, "What if?" For course creator Jenell Stewart, the answer was the freedom to be herself, a new understanding of her value, and the start of a new business.

It started 10 years ago. Just outside a Manhattan night club.

Jenell and her cousin Nenjae walked in; Nenjae turned to Jenell and said: "I'm thinking about going natural with my hair."

"What? You want to do *what*?" Jenell responded. "It was just so foreign to hear that [a decade ago]," she remembers.

Jenell had been chemically relaxing and straightening her hair since she was six years old.

Every eight weeks, for her entire life, she went to the salon or enlisted a relative to apply the chemicals to her scalp that would straighten the roots that grew in.

And while the chemicals are harsh and the process can be—as Jenell shares—painful, she never questioned the routine.

It was all she knew.

It was the *only* option available—or so she thought—for her to feel *beautiful*.

At 25 years old, Jenell had no idea what her natural hair looked like.

So when her cousin told her she was thinking about going natural, Jenell's guttural response was fear.

With the stereotypes that have been ingrained in us for a long, long, long, long time from movies to TV commercials, magazines, books—what we see in the world—it wasn't something that I think a lot of Black women were comfortable doing back then, because we didn't have many examples of what beautiful, natural hair could look like.

Jenell didn't know what she would look like.

She didn't know what her natural hair would feel like.

She didn't know how she would take care of it; at that time it was hard to find products for natural hair.

But Jenell's cousin told her about this small community she'd found on YouTube—women doing what they called The Big Chop: cutting off all their relaxed hair in one swoop to then grow out their natural hair.

These women were recording their experiences in salons and barbershops, and they made videos about their growth process and the new ways they were styling their natural hair.

Despite Jenell's initial fear, she was intrigued.

She'd never even thought she had another choice when it came to her hair. And as scary as it sounded to get to know her natural hair for the first time, it also sounded like a kind of freedom.

As she started to research, she had no idea that such a seemingly small act of curiosity was about to change

more than just her hair. It would change her life.

"COULD THAT BE ME?"

When Jenell got home that night she binged all the YouTube videos where women were documenting their Big Chop.

She was blown away by what she saw.

> *I never knew Black hair could look like that. Could that be me?*

She called her cousin right away. "Let's do it. Let's do it this weekend. I'm going to come over on Friday. You're going to cut my hair, and I'm going to cut yours."

"What?" her cousin replied. "I was planning on transitioning" (i.e., waiting until her new growth was longer before chopping off the relaxed part, to avoid having super-short hair).

Her cousin wanted more time.

But Jenell's enthusiasm convinced her: "Let's do this."

> *I was ready to commit to anything. I just really wanted to be free.*

On March 26, 2010, they got together for their Big Chop. They ordered Chinese food and made toasts; it was a celebration. Then Nenjae cut Jenell's hair, and Jenell cut Nenjae's hair.

> *It was a great experience. We will never forget our Big Chop date*

because it's one of those things that for Black women, that day means so much to you.

(Every year, Jenell and her cousin celebrate March 26 "like a birthday.")

Jenell fell in love with her natural hair and all its possibilities—and she couldn't keep it to herself.

"IT IS SO HARD FOR ME TO KNOW SOMETHING AND NOT TELL PEOPLE."

Jenell started a blog about natural hair the day after her Big Chop and called it *Kinky, Curly, Coily Me.*

"It is so hard for me to know something and not tell people," she explains.

Educating people came naturally (she had a masters degree in education and spent her career thus far as a special education teacher).

People loved Jenell's blog, but readers kept asking her to make video tutorials too.

But Jenell didn't know how to make videos back then.

And she had no video equipment.

But that May, two months after The Big Chop, Jenell's uncle called her.

"Hey, Princess," he said, calling her by her family nickname, "I have a Mac for you."

> ## " I just really wanted to be free.

> # "
> # It was *just* enough for her to keep going.

Jenell felt like "the universe was sending me this Mac." It had iMovie installed.

She started making videos right away.

She laughs as she remembers all the mistakes she made early on, learning how to shoot and edit as she went. But she kept going, studying the videos of those she admired to learn how to get better.

She created nonstop.

And she had no idea who those videos were about to reach.

"OKAY, MAYBE THIS COULD BE A THING."

After almost two years and about 56 videos, the natural hair company SheaMoisture reached out to Jenell. They saw her videos and loved them.

They were looking for ambassadors and started sending her products regularly for her to promote on YouTube.

Then, because she did so well, they asked her to attend events as a SheaMoisture ambassador, flying her out to Virginia to speak.

Jenell thought that sounded fun and agreed. But when she got to the event, she never expected the reception she received. While walking around the event, she would hear people shout:

> *Jenell! I love your channel!*

Then they'd run up and ask if Jenell would take a picture with them. She was floored.

"Who am I that you want to come and take a picture?" she thought.

It was one thing to see views on YouTube. It was another to see shining eyes and hair and hearts coming right up to you.

> *It was just so exciting.*

SheaMoisture paid Jenell for that event, and the amount she made was 5X more than what she made in 40 hours of work at her current day job in education. "I'm in the wrong industry," she started to think.

Around that same time, she became pregnant with her first child.

There were complications.

And after one doctor's appointment, she was put on bedrest.

She wasn't allowed to commute to work.

But she was able to sit at home and make content.

So she did.

For the first time, she experienced what it felt like to dedicate full days to content creation, and as she continued, she started to get that sparkly feeling creators get when momentum builds: "Okay, maybe this could be a thing."

Then her son was born—healthy and happy—but once she returned

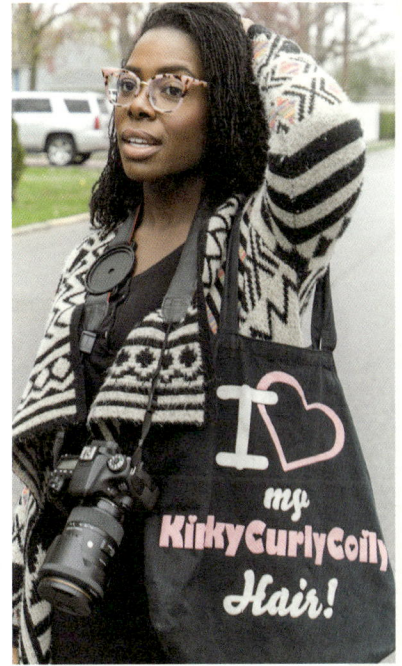

to work after maternity leave, her manager wanted her to take a new job—one with more responsibilities but not more pay.

He was shocked when she turned it down. But the time off had helped her step away from the day job "bubble" and remember who she was and all she had to offer: "In the micro-bubble of everything, sometimes you feel like it's just you and them, and it's not true."

Jenell knew she could get another job if she needed to—but she wanted to take this opportunity to see if she could turn her growing business into something more.

At that same time, other organizations were reaching out to ask her to speak, she started holding her own successful natural hair events, and she was getting sponsorships for her videos.

What if?

She left her job.

With some courage, and a lot of faith:

> *I know that I can make this a legitimate business. I just needed to have the faith to do it. And then, from there, it was just a matter of grinding. Grinding, grinding, grinding, grinding.*

"I HAD A HUNGER IN ME TO MAKE THIS WORK."

The biggest turning point, Jenell explains, was when she started to take herself seriously.

"

—

She started to take herself seriously.

She wasn't going to wait for brands or opportunities to find her. Before she even knew the phrase "media kit," she sent out packages and proposals, showing brands what she could do, who she could reach, and how much it would cost.

> *I was just doing it and putting myself out there, fearlessly and not questioning myself. And not taking it personal if someone said 'No.' Just on to the next one. Because I had a hunger in me to make this work. I have to support my family.*

Her husband's income wasn't enough to keep them afloat. They kept their expenses low, but she knew she needed to make money soon or she'd have to find another job right away.

But for every 20 no's, there was a yes.

During the first year working on her business full-time, she made about half of what she made at her old job; but because they kept their expenses low, it was just enough for her to keep going.

She loved the work, and she loved being home with her son.

And she knew that even if she hadn't met her full-time financial goals yet, the part-time income was proof that there was potential. This was possible.

She just needed to leverage the potential that was already there.

And that's when she started dedicating herself to learning online marketing.

"WHY WOULD WE NOT SPEND THAT IN ANY ENDEAVOR IN LIFE?"

Jenell is her own best example of what it looks like to take online marketing education seriously.

> *I was always reading blogs about how to blog. I was always watching YouTube videos about how to YouTube. I was always reading books.*

She saw too many people confuse the access of the internet with ease of building an audience. She was shocked to learn how some people think you can transition to a career in content creation and make money instantly, without education.

> *When you think about what we spend in time and money for college, why would we not spend that in any endeavor in life?*

Jenell focused on finding people who taught online marketing whom she trusted, people who were experts in the field. She listened to their podcasts. Attended their webinars. Joined their email lists.

That's when she learned about online courses and how email and webinars could be a great way to sell them.

She loved that YouTube sent an email to everyone subscribed to her channel when a new video came out—but what about all the people watching her videos who weren't subscribed?

And she didn't think pitching a $1,000 course made sense via a YouTube video.

YouTube and social media would be perfect for getting people on her email list, and then email is where she would build trust and sell her course.

She used lots of opt-ins to build her email list, and still does: "I have tons of landing pages."

Jenell dedicated two years to her own kind of self-created online business MBA. But instead of *owing* tens of thousands of dollars by the end of those two years, Jenell had a business that was now consistently making over six figures.

The last hurdle she would have to face was understanding that she was indeed worth six figures.

"MAKING A YOUTUBE VIDEO IS LIKE MAKING A PEANUT BUTTER AND JELLY SANDWICH."

Once Jenell hit six figures in her business, she was elated, but she was also fearful. She had imposter syndrome and struggled to believe she was really worth what brands were paying her, "Because what I do comes to me so easy, I sometimes feel like I have to overcompensate."

If a brand asked her to make a video for $1,000, she would offer three videos, because making one video felt too "easy" to her: "To me, making a YouTube video is like making a peanut butter and jelly sandwich."

She didn't feel right charging someone so much for something that came so easily.

She feared that if she didn't include a ton of other services along with the video, then brands wouldn't take her seriously, even though she knew she had the numbers to validate the reach and value one video could provide; she just struggled to believe she was really worth it.

Like when she got hired by Nissan to do an Instagram story takeover at an event in Manhattan. "I got in my head so much," she remembers.

She spent hours trying to get the perfect image, terrified every time she sent a new photo or video to the person at Nissan in charge of approving the content, thinking it wouldn't be good enough.

But every time she sent an image, Nissan replied back, instantly: "Love it, post it."

Their positive response finally helped her see what was there all along.

BUSINESS BY THE NUMBERS

4,040	→	EMAIL LIST SUBSCRIBERS
20%	→	AVERAGE OPEN RATE
93%	→	AVERAGE CLICK RATE
3M	→	EMAILS SENT

REVENUE BREAKDOWN

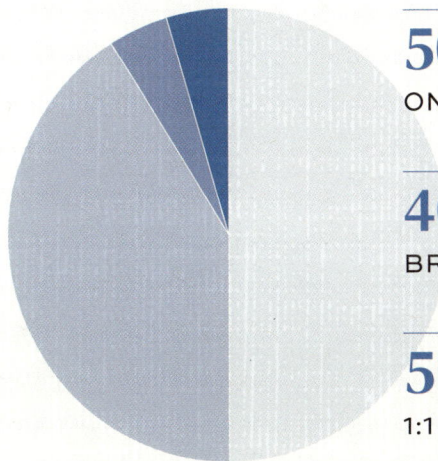

50%
ONLINE COURSE SALES

40%
BRAND PARTNERSHIPS

5%
1:1 COACHING

5%
GOOGLE ADS

You can offer more to them.

I have the audience, I have the engagement, I have the experience, and they're coming to me; I shouldn't feel like I can't ask for what I want.

That has changed my life.

Once she tackled her imposter syndrome and started appreciating what she was worth, her income tripled.

"IT'S STILL CRAZY TO ME."

Jenell, the former teacher, can't believe her life sometimes.

I'm a very by-the-book kind of person, so being in the field that I'm in, it's still crazy to me.

Since her early natural hair blog days 10 years ago, she's expanded into all kinds of content topics. She's still that same enthusiastic woman who always wants to share what she's learning with others.

When she had a daughter and her fans, who were also having daughters of their own, asked if she would teach them how to do their daughters' natural hair, she said yes.

Today, Jenell has a YouTube channel with her own daughter Elle. Together they show moms and their children that they have choices—that who they are is beautiful, and that the possibilities, for their hair and their futures, are endless. ■

They hired me because I'm good at this. Why am I making it seem like I don't deserve to be here?

She started educating herself on her particular brand of imposter syndrome and realized:

I was undermining my gift.

When you first start out doing something, you charge a little bit because you're not that good. But would you charge even less when you got faster or better at doing it?

No, you don't charge less.

You charge more because you're better at it.

WEB DESIGNER + PRODUCT PHOTOGRAPHER

ITSPINKPOT.COM

The beautiful side of failure

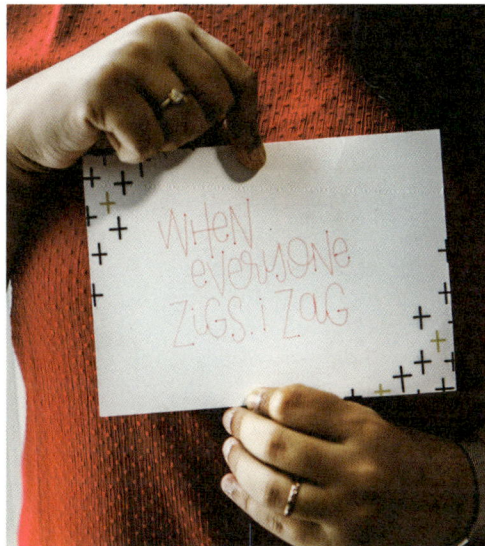

Moments of crisis are where we find our true and inherent resolve. When faced with actual failure, web designer Chaitra Radhakrishna didn't let fear slow her down.

It happened at 3:00 a.m. Chaitra called her boyfriend, waking him up, euphoric: *"I think I know what I want to do in my life."*

It all started with beauty bloggers, her first "friends" after leaving her home of Bangalore, India, to move to the U.S. for a job. Home alone at night, she watched YouTube beauty tutorials.

But Chaitra craved her own creative outlet and started a beauty blog as a hobby in 2013. She called it *Pinkpot*, and it took off.

But not at all in the way she expected.

People were responding to Chaitra's content—but they weren't asking about hair and makeup. They wanted to know how she made her *photos* look so great and what she was using for her blog design.

With a master's degree in computer science, Chaitra knew how to code and was "a bit of a fanatic for design and photography; my whole *goal* was to make it look good."

She started answering people's design questions. It energized her.

She'll never forget how shocked she was to see a time on the clock that she'd never seen before: 3:00 a.m. Chaitra says she is known for falling asleep early, always in bed by 11:00 p.m. "Nothing can ever keep me up at night—not a good movie, not anything."

Until she started helping people with blog design.

A creator knows she's found her craft when time itself disappears.

She had no idea how to pursue what she was doing as a job, but she couldn't keep the feeling to herself and called her boyfriend at 3:00 a.m to share the revelation.

"NINE-TO-FIVE JOB PEOPLE."

For seven months, Chaitra worked as an academic researcher by day and blogger by night. She wanted to pursue her blog as more than a hobby, but she was nervous: "How would I bring in money?"

She started researching all the ways you could monetize a blog and chose her favorite—making her own products. She created five website templates and sold them for $30 each.

Her first goal? Make $500 a month.

She made $760 that first month, February 2015. She still cites it as her dream-come-true moment: "It was so special. That first sale, nothing can match that, you know?"

By the end of 2015, she was making $2,000 each month.

Her research job was also progressing. Both were taking up a lot of time and energy and she wasn't sure how long she could do both at the same level. The university was offering

> **Nobody can tell you if something is going to work or not because they don't know either.**

> ## " Make the pros and cons list, then throw it away and do what you feel like doing.

her advancement, and her blog was requiring more, too. She had to make a choice on what would come first: Go all in on the blog or the academic career path?

One was risky.

One was safe, nine-to-five.

Her parents, she tells me, were very much "nine-to-five job people." Security, saving, and not taking risks were key tenets of their unspoken family motto. Chaitra understood completely where her loving parents were coming from, though. They

had "a more challenging upbringing. They just wanted to be safe and protect us."

She also liked the research job. Struggling inside her own head to make a decision, she asked her 3:00 am-boyfriend-now-husband for his advice. Knowing how much she liked to make pros and cons lists, he said:

> *Make the pros and cons list, then throw it away and do what you feel like doing.*

She went full-time on her blog in August 2015. It was a big risk, but one she was excited about. At least for a while.

It didn't take long for the fear of failure to follow.

"THERE IS NO CLEAR FORMULA THAT TELLS YOU 'THIS WILL WORK.'"

The reality of the big change she made hit her later: "I always grew up with this mind-set of I'm going to work nine-to-five. Entrepreneurship is not for 'people like us,' because we don't believe in taking risks. I was really scared."

The steady beat of her old paycheck was replaced with, *"What if this doesn't work?"*

The fear slowed her down in the beginning. "I feel like I would have done it faster if I didn't give that fear importance." She tried to plan everything out perfectly—reduce the risk—trying to make sure that everything she tried "would definitely work" before taking the next step.

But the doubt-induced-slowness started to irritate her. Sick of her own paralyzing fear, she realized she was chasing after a kind of security that didn't exist. "There is no clear formula that tells you 'This will work.' I was just wasting time."

She learned how to recognize her hyper-planning and false-security-chasing modes in the moment, stopping them like a state trooper pulling over a car that's driving under the speed limit.

Her fear of failure was finally under control. Until she was faced with actual failure.

"IT STILL FAILED."

It started with the failure of the DSLR camera she was renting from the university in her early blogging days. It broke during a brand photo shoot and she had no other choice but to use her iPhone to take the pictures. To her surprise, and the brand's, the photos came out great.

She started using her iPhone for all her blog photos, and her audience was shocked (and excited) by what she was doing. With her first iPhone stock photography pack growing her email list like crazy, she got an idea: *What if I built a course that taught people how to take their own great photos with their iPhone?*

She did a beta test of the course, offering 10 spots with a 50% discount to her email list. The beta response was great—so great that she had to rush to close the cart when she realized 16 people had purchased. They loved the course, and with such a successful beta, Chaitra couldn't wait to see what would happen when she launched it to a wider audience and at full price. "I had huge expectations."

But when she launched her course in November 2016, "the response was very cold. I had not expected it at all."

expect, you start taking it very personally. *"Oh I did something wrong. Or maybe my customers don't like me. Maybe my customers don't like the course I created."*

And then, the ringer:

Maybe people just don't think I'm good enough.

But such crises of confidence, if allowed but not gripped, often make space for new resolve. "So this is what failure looks like," Chaitra said to herself after the tears dried, "This is what you were fearing, and it's not too bad. It's not too bad at all." She'd survived.

Her new plan? "Go see why it failed."

All those ugly voices she was reacting to were really only in her head. No one had actually said any of those things to her. She realized if she dove a little deeper she could focus on what actually needed fixing.

The more she separated herself from the failure, from the event, from even the course itself, the more empowered she felt as a creator.

Because, after all, she was the only one with the power to fix this, to find a solution and try again.

She was dejected and confused. The failure seemed to confirm her worst fears. She researched. She planned. She tested. "It still failed."

She was left alone with the question all creators must face at some point:

What went wrong?

"GO SEE WHY IT FAILED."

It's not a question that has to be answered right away. For most creators, grieving must come first.

I cried for a couple days. When something doesn't go the way you

"ALL YOU CAN DO IS KEEP EXPERIMENTING."

Chaitra dedicated the next three months to putting on her research hat once more, interviewing those who bought the course and those who didn't, studying her course launch emails, and trying to figure out what went wrong.

She found three problems—and three solutions, which she implemented right away.

PROBLEM 1: She didn't spend enough time on the launch details.

She got so wrapped up in creating the course that she neglected putting the same time and attention into the copywriting and strategy that go into a product launch. People clearly loved the course and found it wildly helpful— the problem wasn't with the course. It was with the launch.

SOLUTION 1: Put the same time and energy she put into the course content into the launch content.

PROBLEM 2: The first launch emails were all about her.

Her first launch emails talked mostly about the course curriculum and what excited her about the course. The emails didn't spend enough time answering the only question that really mattered: How would the course make a difference in the businesses and lives of the students?

SOLUTION 2: She rewrote her entire email launch sequence to focus only on how the course could help someone's business. Then, she laid

BUSINESS BY THE NUMBERS

9,146 → EMAIL LIST SUBSCRIBERS

40% → AVERAGE OPEN RATE

50,000 → MONTHLY PAGEVIEWS

REVENUE BREAKDOWN

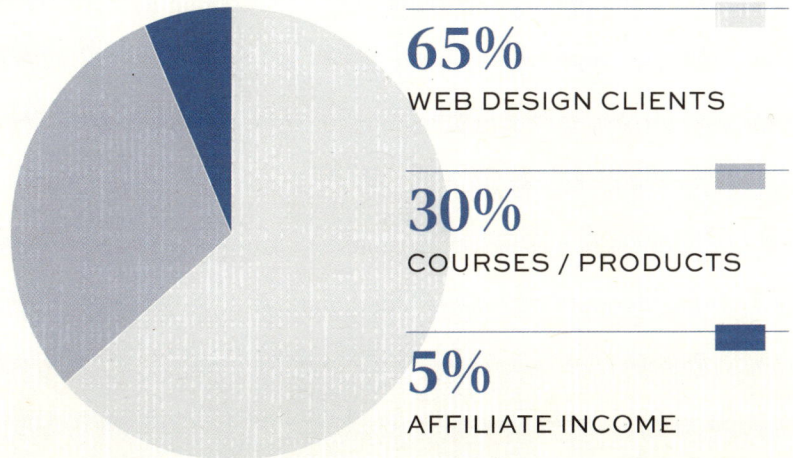

65%
WEB DESIGN CLIENTS

30%
COURSES / PRODUCTS

5%
AFFILIATE INCOME

out in great detail who the course was right for and who it wasn't right for. Her emails had an educational tone, but this time, instead of teaching them what was in the course, she focused on teaching them how the course would help.

PROBLEM 3: Some people could afford $97 but couldn't afford $197.

To encourage students to buy the beta course, she'd offered it for $97—half price. But when it came time to launch the course at full price, she heard crickets. While most weren't ready to make the investment because they didn't yet understand how the course would add value back into their lives and businesses, there were a select few who simply did not have that kind of money to invest in their business right now.

SOLUTION 3: Chaitra created a second pricing tier with a pared down version of the course to provide support to those who couldn't afford to spend more than $100.

She launched the course again, with a big goal of getting 100 students.

She got 250.

Even though Chaitra's first launch "failed" in her eyes, it was actually the perfect way to start. Jumping in before things were "perfect" is what generated the data she needed to make the second launch a success.

> # A creator knows she's found her craft when time itself disappears.

Nobody can tell you if something is going to work or not because they don't know either. All you can do is keep experimenting—trial and error. Keep tweaking, see how people respond, and keep going.

I realized what failure actually looks like and that it's nothing to be fearful about. I think the best way to get over failure is just go face it. Let it happen; let something not go the way you expected.

"FEEL THE FEAR AND DO IT ANYWAY."

That's not to say facing her fears is ever easy.

Later when Chaitra was asked to speak at AltSummit, a well-known blogger conference, she was terrified—but not of public speaking.

She was terrified of her own voice.

"I was always conscious about my accent; I was really nervous somehow people would not understand what I was trying to say." But her desire to connect was greater than her fear. It

While she often felt different, she realized she was far from alone.

would be the first time she'd take her business outside her house.

She showed up, hoping her presentation would make a difference, even if only one or two people understood her.

The audience response changed her forever.

People lined up to thank her. She remembers with great joy how some even said, "Your accent is so cute." She was embraced. It gave her new confidence, along with a new creator's creed: "Just be you and it's going to be great."

Chaitra shared her revelation on Instagram a few weeks later and people commented like crazy, sharing their own stories of insecurity and ambition, thanking her for the courage to own her beautiful, perfect voice.

While she often felt different, she realized she was far from alone.

On the other side of her fears was the kind of community and contribution she'd been dreaming of when she moved to a new country by herself. The gains were always so much greater than the losses she'd imagine in her head.

You're not gonna lose anything by trying. So just go ahead and try it out. It's totally okay if you fail; the bigger failure is thinking one day, "What if I'd tried?"

The other side of failure, Chaitra says, is "beautiful. Even if it doesn't work out. So what! You at least tried, right? You at least know that you gave it your all. Be courageous and go for it. Feel the fear and do it anyway." ■

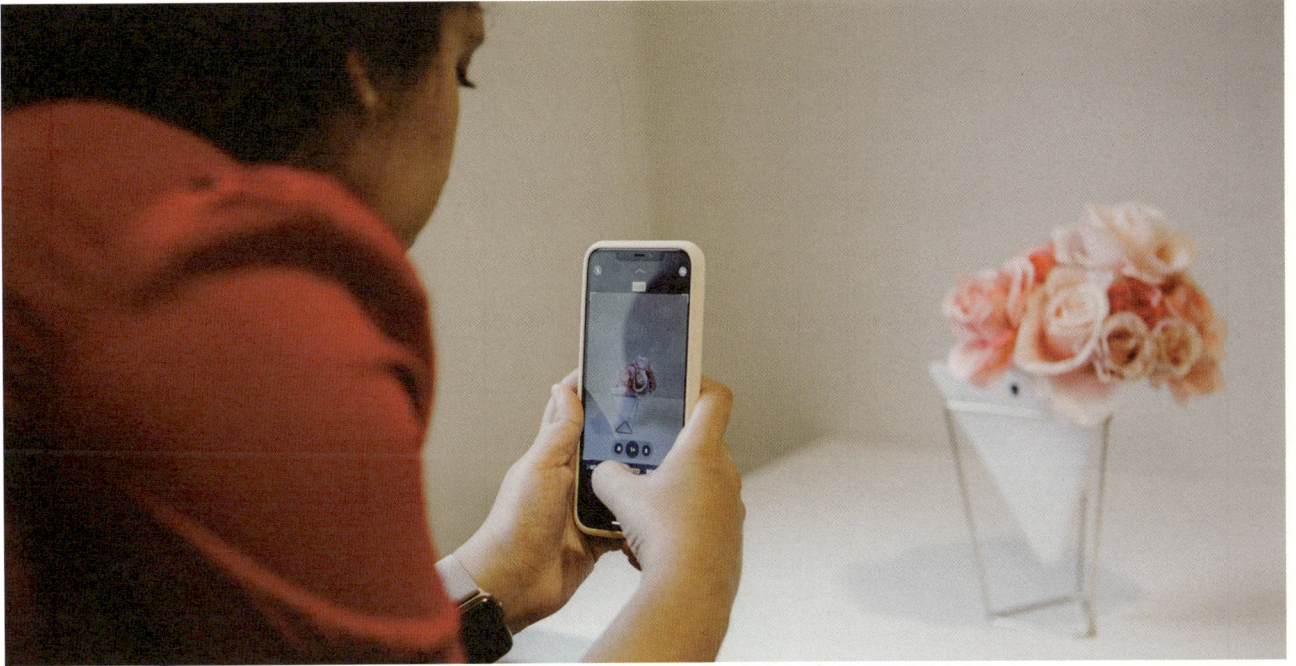

Proof of a life fully lived

Trauma and chronic illness. Writer Jessica Bird has known too much of both in her young life. This is her story of overcoming the unexpected, finding confidence, and how a conference opened her eyes to endless possiblities.

I'm freezing. I don't know why I didn't think to bring a warmer jacket to the Oregon coast in October. I blame it on my having only ever lived in sunny places—Florida and California. But now I'm on the beach in Florence, Oregon, getting pelted by icy rain because the winds blew back my turquoise umbrella, rendering it useless.

To my left walks Jessica Bird on a sand dune, umbrella-less, wearing a knit maroon hat and an open smile. This is her happy place. She always dreamed of living by the ocean in Florence, and just a few weeks ago she made that dream come true—coming to Florence with nothing but her newly purchased RV and some bravery.

A few hours earlier she emailed me about our potential rainy ocean walk:

I've come to realize I'm freakin' crazy and most people don't enjoy standing in the cold wet wind to stare at the misty ocean haze— and I know you have warm ocean views at home—so I promise not to be offended if you don't want to join me!

But this is my first time in Oregon and I've never stood on its coast nor walked on the beach in the rain, so I say yes.

There are seagulls everywhere. They don't mind the rain at all. Jessica tells me about the dead seagull she found on the beach once. An off-leash dog started running toward it and she got worried; but after the dog sniffed, it simply curled up beside the motionless bird.

In the next four hours I spend with Jessica we talk about her new (and thriving) service business, why she decided to move to Florence even though she knows no one here, and what it's like living with Cystic Fibrosis (CF). We also talk a lot about trauma, forgiveness, her 10 miscarriages, and her "fur babies"—the animals she rescued, each one after a miscarriage.

It's hard enough to survive the ups and downs of running a business. So how do you survive when you also have to deal with the unexpected and undeserved things life can throw at you, like chronic illness and trauma?

"I WANT THEM TO KNOW I WAS HERE."

Jessica's mom was 16 years old when she had Jessica. She knew right away that something wasn't right—her daughter was sick. But everyone brushed her off, saying that Jessica's coughing was normal, that her lungs were still growing, that she'd be just fine.

Then, during one hospital visit, a nurse kissed baby Jessica on the head and noticed she tasted salty. "Has she been tested for CF?" the nurse asked. Cystic Fibrosis causes the body to produce more salt, Jessica explains.

Jessica has been living with Cystic Fibrosis her entire life. She tells me how her best friend in high school was 76 years old, and it doesn't occur to me until I'm in a long taxi ride to the airport, passing mossy scrub

trees that look like fairy homes, that Jessica's Cystic Fibrosis could mean that her own vibrant red hair may never turn gray.

Tomorrow is Jessica's birthday. She'll turn 24, and she's very excited about it.

I know that my disease will likely lead to a slow death. I could suffocate in my own lungs or struggle along for months and years as my organs slowly shut down. Or if I'm a lucky duck I might even live long enough to die of colon cancer. So... that's terrifying.

Except it's not really.

Jessica's business (and writings) keep her focused on what really matters to her.

Her business, her online presence, her being a creator, isn't really about money for her.

I want them to know I was here.

Before she had her own business, Jessica worked as a healthcare assistant. It was going fine—until she started getting too sick to come into work. She felt so guilty when her health declined—she'd been praised in the past for being so well despite having CF. When things started to get bad, she took it personally.

She had to make choices that no one should have to make. She chose her health, but it resulted in her losing her job.

> ## " You don't need to apologize; you're doing perfect.

But then she panicked. It felt too good to be true. She didn't think she deserved it.

A week later, everything fell apart. She had to be hospitalized. Her husband got pneumonia. Her apartment changed their policy and she had to get rid of one of her dogs. They received a $10,000 bill for her hospital stay that they couldn't afford.

That's when Jessica started her first business; she had to be able to work from home. She read "every blog on the planet" about online business, hired a business coach, and got to work. Within a few months she was making a full-time living working from home as a coach and an author.

But then she panicked. It felt too good to be true. She didn't think she deserved it.

Her traumatic childhood coupled with growing up poor left her with money issues; making money freaked her out.

Instead of seeing that she was helping people and that her clients were telling her they were getting more from her than they were paying for, all she could see was the "taking" people's money part. She knew what it felt like to struggle financially, and having other people give her their precious money became too much. She froze and closed her business, even deleting her first email list.

"DON'T CRY, DON'T CRY. I'M FINE, I'M FINE."

To make ends meet, she started looking for design jobs on Upwork (her first business revealed she had a real talent for Canva and graphic design). Creators like Annie LaCroix, the host of the Brainy Boss podcast, started hiring Jessica to help them with their businesses.

Jessica remembers apologizing to Annie a lot in the beginning, still raw from the shame of her first business shut-down. Annie responded with the same message every time: "You don't need to apologize; you're doing perfect."

Annie had no idea she would change Jessica's life with her kindness: "She helped me regain my confidence. She really saw me." In 2019, Annie invited Jessica to come to our Craft + Commerce conference. She even bought Jessica's ticket.

"I was so scared," Jessica remembers. The first half of 2019 had left Jessica reeling from acute trauma that had caused her to become suicidal. "I wanted to die every day. I had plans. It was horrible. It was a really, really bad time."

Jessica remembers walking into Craft + Commerce feeling like "a raw wound, where the skin is hanging by

a thread and everything that brushes up against it stings."

What she didn't expect was how the creators she met would become a salve.

> I felt so alone in the world, all by myself. And then, I'm at this place where there's so much love and connection. And all these people are actually doing what I was scared to even believe I could do.

She was also blown away by how much fun everyone seemed to be having. "I'd never met people who were just creative for the fun of it."

Most of all, she was mesmerized by the idea that business didn't have to be cold, sleazy—take, take, take. It was the first time she'd ever been surrounded by people who, like her, cared more about what they could give than what they would get.

During one of the last sessions of the first day it all started to hit her: the possibility, the unique comfort she was finding amongst creators, and the quiet voice telling her that

> "
> ———
>
> I felt so alone in the world, all by myself. And then, I'm at this place where there's so much love and connection.

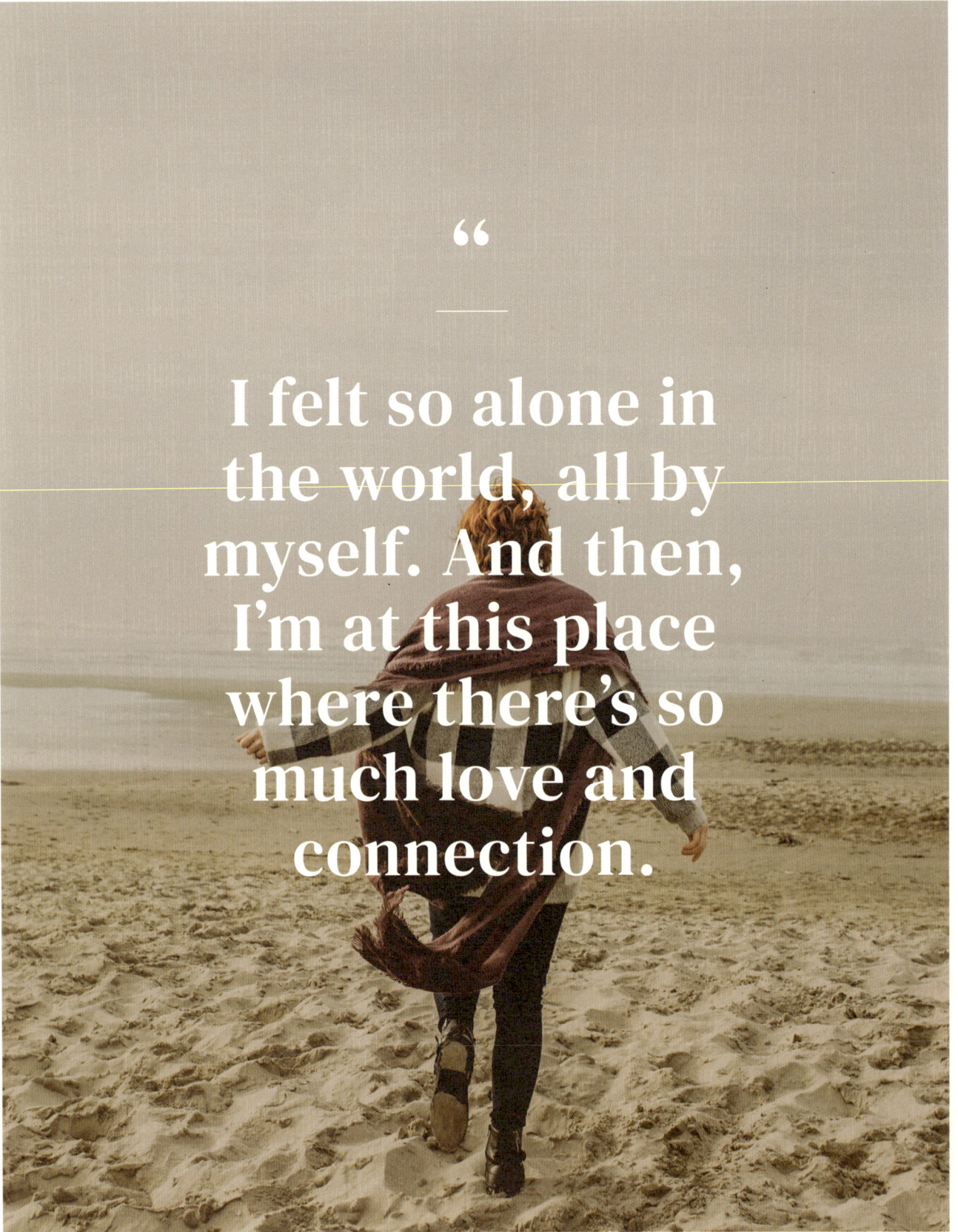

she belonged here, that she was a creator too.

Her eyes started to water.

Annie saw and patted her shoulder. But Jessica didn't want to fall apart in the conference session. She kept this mantra going in her head: "Don't cry, don't cry, don't cry, don't cry. I'm fine, I'm fine, I'm fine, I'm fine."

She made it. She didn't cry. The session let out to a coffee break where Jessica started to observe all the friendly creators talking passionately about their work. "Everybody was just glowing."

But those tears she pushed down weren't going to stay away for much longer. She couldn't deny her feelings anymore. The very fact that she was feeling anything was enough to make her cry.

"I HADN'T FELT ANYTHING FOR SO LONG."

She couldn't hold it in anymore, and she didn't want to be alone. She looked around for a familiar face and spotted Alexis, Craft + Commerce's emcee. Jessica walked up to Alexis to express her appreciation for the conference, but all she got out was "Can I…" and then she wept in Alexis' arms.

I ask Jessica why she still has her Craft + Commerce badge displayed prominently in her living area, nestled amongst her most precious paintings, letters, poems, and pictures.

I had this version of business in my head where everybody who makes money is selfish and stubborn and in a hurry—everything I can't stand. But Craft + Commerce didn't feel like that.

For someone who has Cystic Fibrosis, the concept of hurrying through life is appalling. Jessica savors. I think back to our slow drive to her RV earlier when she told me, laughingly, her response to people who seem annoyed that she drives too slow: "I can't be hurried."

She stares at her Craft + Commerce lanyard whenever she feels alone or notices those old money-myths creeping in. The badge reminds her that while she may be alone in Florence right now, she's connected to creators around the world who care as much as she does about craft, and who pursue commerce from a place of generosity, not greed.

The creators she met—their acceptance, their kindness—changed her.

For me, being kind is the most important thing because you don't know what people are going through. I'm the bubbliest person on the planet and I've been raped twice and I've had 10 miscarriages and I've lost people I loved. And you'd never know that by looking at me.

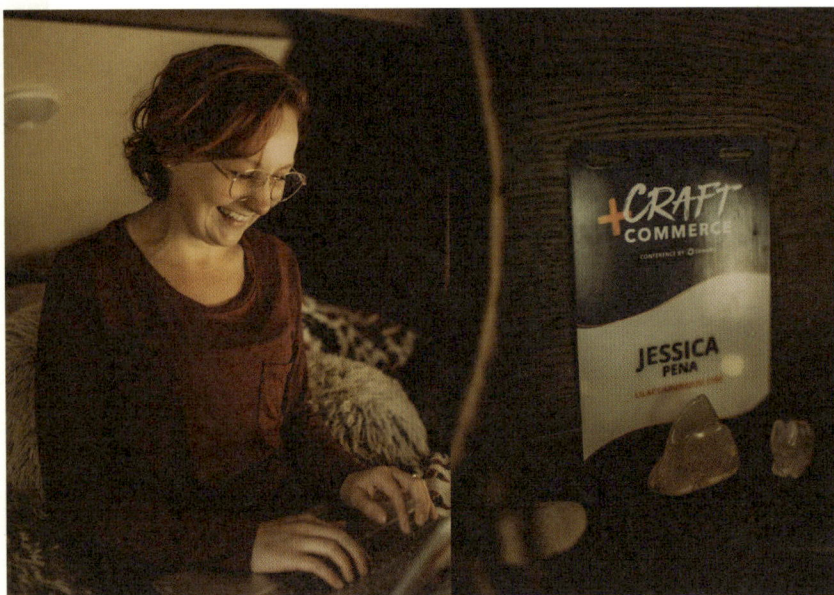

"Because I'm not that good," Jessica answered.

The designer smiled in recognition and shared her own experience: "I've been doing this for 12 years and I still don't feel like an expert." She told Jessica how she approaches every new job with a sense of, "I don't know if I'm a good enough web designer for this, but I can try."

This designer, Jessica tells me, is amazing at her craft, and she showed Jessica that you could still try and take steps—even when you're feeling doubtful—and that no matter how much experience you have, you might never feel like you know it all. And maybe that's the point.

The more she got to know the creators at the conference, the more Jessica realized everyone struggled with self-doubt; no one felt like they had it all together or knew what they were doing all the time. They almost never felt "ready."

"Wait, that's how everybody feels?" she remembers thinking. It was a revelation.

After the first night of the conference, she built a brand-new website and started her second business: Revived Socials.

And because almost everyone exchanges emails with the creators they connect with at the conference, by the end of weekend, six people had emailed her asking if they could hire her.

At Craft + Commerce I realized that all these people making money were not heartless, evil monsters. They had so much love. They were so human. It was the first time I saw up close that money doesn't ruin everything.

Those creators at the conference were equally impressed by her and her design skills.

They showed me that I was actually really good at graphic design and social media management.

At one of the pre-conference meetups for web designers, feeling very shy and unworthy, Jessica did not introduce herself as a designer. She remembers when one designer, after seeing Jessica's work, incredulously asked, "Why didn't you say you were a designer?"

By her second month, she had contracts totaling $3,000 a month.

She did that with a tiny email list, too.

I built this business on a community of creators, from a space of generosity. It turns out even strangers will support you and spread your message like wildfire when you show up with your whole heart and a plan to truly serve. The real power isn't in the number of followers you have; it's in the quality of the relationships you have.

"REST AND LET IT BE ENOUGH"

Jessica and I finish the delicious tortellini tomato soup she made for me and decide to go to a nearby coffee shop to finish our chat because I am starting to sniffle (I'm sadly allergic to dogs and cats).

As I gather my things, I take in the cozy RV—fairy lights, a 2018 and 2019 vision board (both featuring pictures of the ocean), fresh pink flowers, three purple potatoes and four red apples on the tiny kitchen counter, and a bag of cardamom that she tells me takes the acidity out of coffee.

I also notice a "Create Every Day" sticker on the laptop where she does all her business and her writing; she sees Revived Socials as the day job she's created for herself to support her writing. Her blog, *The Serendipity Lifestyle*, is an inspiration to many

BUSINESS BY THE NUMBERS

108 → EMAIL LIST SUBSCRIBERS

44% → AVERAGE OPEN RATE

REVENUE BREAKDOWN

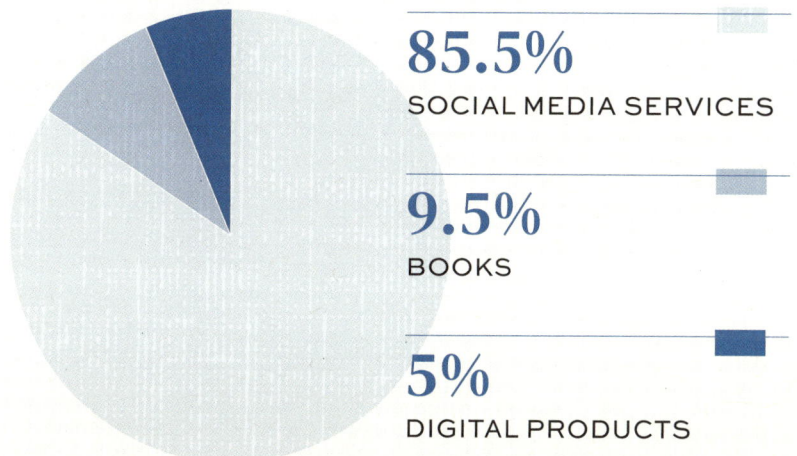

85.5%
SOCIAL MEDIA SERVICES

9.5%
BOOKS

5%
DIGITAL PRODUCTS

and she gets up at 5:30 a.m to write her books.

Before we go, I ask Jessica one last question: "What advice would you share with creators who are dealing with chronic health issues that might be interfering with their stamina or routine, or who perhaps feel weighed down by trauma but don't want to lose their big dreams?"

She responds immediately: "It's super easy to say and super hard to do." She takes a breath and shares the advice she's always trying to take herself: "Rest and let it be enough."

After she takes each dog out one by one on a leash (they are so tiny that they spend most of their time outside beneath the shelter of the RV, staying out of the rain), we head to the coffee shop where, after I order a chai, she orders a "pumpkin chai" and I turn to her and say "Wait a minute—where is that on the menu? I must have missed it."

"No, you didn't miss it." When she first moved to Florence—a longtime dream of hers—it was fall and she wanted pumpkin spice, but not coffee. She asked if they could add pumpkin to her chai, and they said yes.

I change my order to a "pumpkin chai" and stand outside with her in the rain (I leave my umbrella behind this time). I take in the water view behind the café as I sip my pumpkin chai (it's delicious), and Jessica tells me about how this exact view is what made her decide to move to Florence. It's lonely sometimes, and she has no idea what will happen next, but she takes all that in as proof that she is alive. ∎

CHAPTER TWO

Quitting your job

"I QUIT."

It's a moment a lot of people dream about—walking out of their day jobs and into sunshine and rainbows.

But quitting a job is not where any of the stories in this chapter end— it's where they begin.

And none of these creators really hated their day jobs, either. More often than not, their day job was a springboard, a learning ground, a motivator.

None of these quitting stories are the same; some quit in a flash, while others phased out, slowly in whatever way made sense for them and their family.

Being a creator is a job, too, just one where you're more in control. Creating your own job comes with its own challenges—it's not always easy. But it's almost always exhilarating.

To be happy now

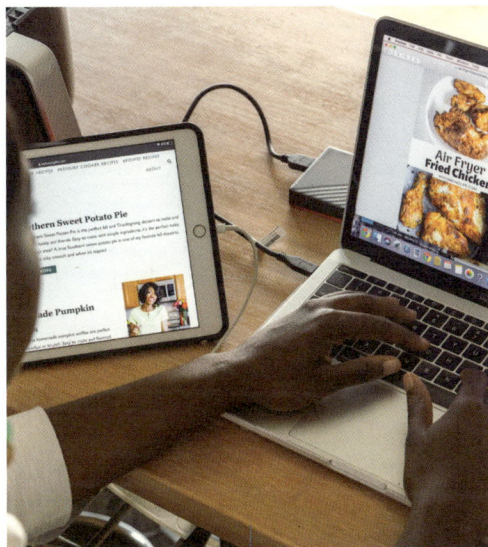

It only took five months for Tanya Harris' blog income to match her lawyer's salary. But while filling her bank account month after month by talking about food was exciting, she needed to dig deep into her own resolve to take the full-time leap.

PHOTOGRAPHY BY → JEROME STOCKTON FLEMING II

Tanya Harris lights up when talking through writing her first blog post about getting the fishy taste out of catfish:

> *I really enjoyed it. I don't think anyone read it, but I loved the feeling of creating something. It was fun.*

Fun. No one talks about fun in blogging anymore. Growth and traffic and content, oh my.

All of that is important, but it's not where it has to start.

Fun is a great place to start. So is purpose. And quiet. A deliberate quieting —of all the noise— so you can hear your own voice.

The internet is crowded; it's hard to hear (or trust) your voice. It's hard to believe there's room.

But there isn't just room, there's hunger—people are tired of the formulas and are starving for content that comes from the deepest places of a creator's heart.

When I walk into Tanya's North Carolina home, it's hard to tell where the kitchen ends and the rest of the house begins. It's wide and open and full—almost every inch of counter is taken up with fresh vegetables from her husband's garden or some kind of air fryer or pressure cooker.

(The official report is that Tanya has three pressure cookers and five air fryers—though her nine-year-old daughter informs me that the more accurate number of air fryers she has is "a thousand.")

We sit down at a wooden table in the kitchen, and while it rains and the peaches defrost for a cobbler Tanya is going to make me soon, I ask her when she fell in love with food and how it led to quitting her job as a lawyer just a few months ago.

"THIS IS EDIBLE."

The taste and creativity of a meal wasn't part of Tanya's life growing up; meals were just another box to check on a long to-do list.

"My mom is Jamaican, but she didn't always cook Jamaican food." Why? Because, as Tanya explains, she was busy. She was a nurse who fed her kids whatever was quick, easy, and nourishing, where "recipes" involved only one to two steps, like: "defrost chicken" (now-foodie Tanya tries not to shudder at the memory). For the majority of her early life, work came before cooking.

"When I was in college and law school, I was a terrible cook and had no passion to make good food." Her only criteria? "This is edible."

But in 2012, a book changed Tanya's food life.

While wandering around a local bookstore, a cookbook caught her eye: *How to Cook Everything* by Mark Bittman.

The author made cooking accessible, even for someone with no experience. "This man teaches you how to make scrambled eggs! And I loved the step-by-step photos."

She bought the book and made scrambled eggs that night; it changed her outlook on food forever.

You can make really good food if you actually try!

She fell in love with cooking. She bought more cookbooks. She followed food bloggers. But she never imagined she'd become one.

"I'm not like most people. I didn't hate my job." But by 2016, Tanya had been a lawyer for seven years. She found herself yearning for a fresh challenge, for something outside work and family—something of her own.

She started her food blog in March 2016 as a way to share the joy happening in her kitchen.

When she first launched, she didn't have many readers or comments—but she had a lot of fun.

"I WAS TIRED."

However, after the first year, she decided to take a break from blogging.

"Why?" I ask.

"I was tired." She answers simply and confidently. I smile in understanding, one overachieving creator to another.

> ## "
> # The internet is crowded; it's hard to hear (or trust) your voice. It's hard to believe there's room.

Tanya had good reason to be tired.

She and her husband had been going through the intensive in-vitro process for months in hopes to have a second child. Struggling through the physical and emotional roller coaster that is IVF, in addition to working full-time and caring for her daughter, was draining. Tanya simply didn't have anything left. She pressed pause on the blog.

Then one day before her next scheduled treatment, she bought an over-the-counter pregnancy test. "There was the faintest line. I actually walked into the appointment the next day and let them know I was pregnant!"

And with that pregnancy came the cravings—particularly the french fry cravings.

> *We had a deep fryer at home, but since I was pregnant, I wanted to eat healthy for myself and the baby. I was in an aisle of a store rubbing my belly when I saw two air fryers sitting on the display shelf.*

"I'm not like most people. I didn't hate my job."

They were all coming from a pressure cooker shrimp paella recipe she'd shared before she pressed pause.

People weren't just raving about the recipes either, they were also asking her follow-up questions. They wanted her help. *How do you use a pressure cooker exactly? What do you do if you have one of the smaller ones? What if you can't find saffron?*

Those questions launched her business because she desperately wanted to answer them. She couldn't *not* answer them. She became obsessed with the idea that she could help people around the world. Her purpose expanded; it wasn't just about her anymore. And that was the moment everything changed. She started to dream about quitting her job to do this full-time.

"IT'S NOT JUST MY BLOG; IT'S MY BUSINESS."

As a lawyer and former collegiate track athlete, Tanya knew she wouldn't make money blogging

> *I was contemplating whether or not I should get one when a lady walked right up and grabbed one and walked away. So I grabbed the other one and bought it.*

That air fryer kept her in endlessly easy fries all throughout her pregnancy. She was happy.

Maybe food didn't have to be tied to blogging. Maybe food would be something she enjoyed privately.

But the blog wasn't ready to say goodbye.

Tanya kept getting email alerts that people were commenting on the blog—*every* day there were more and more. She hadn't been thinking about the blog, but she was curious. *What are all these people commenting about?*

simply by wishing it so. She got to work.

Step one? Podcasts.

I got obsessed.

She listened to podcasts anytime she was in the car: driving to work, running errands, taking her daughter to school. Her daughter used to complain (she preferred music), but eventually, she got it.

"Oh, you're doing this for your blog," Tanya remembers her daughter saying in the car a few weeks after the podcast binge began.

"Yeah, I'm trying to learn. And it's not just my blog, it's my *business*."

Those podcasts taught Tanya how SEO and Google Analytics could help more people find her blog. With her new metrics mindset, she started researching her blog's traffic and found that, on average, she was getting about 2,000 views a month (after the shrimp paella recipe went viral, it jumped to 7,000).

The podcasts also referenced the ad network Mediavine a lot. She signed up, set a goal of 25,000 unique visitors in one month, and got back into the kitchen.

"I WANTED TO BE HAPPY NOW. NOT TWO YEARS FROM NOW."

Tanya started making more recipes with her air fryer. So far she'd only used it to make her beloved french fries, and it seemed like a waste of a big gadget to only serve her fries frenzy. So she started experimenting.

And it worked. Her SEO and Google Trends research also confirmed that air fryers were having a bit of a "moment."

People were flocking to her site.

People were making her food.

People were clicking on the ads.

Tanya's blog started to make money.

I remember when I made my first $10. I immediately told my husband: "I made $10!" I was really excited.

She was hooked. And she made a declaration in the summer of 2018:

In a year I want to quit my job and do this full-time.

She told some friends who were supportive enough but not super interested. The pact was really to herself, and she started getting even more strategic, working on weekends and every lunch break—a total of 15 hours per week.

It was intense, but it paid off. In December of 2018, just five months after her summer declaration, Tanya's blog income matched her lawyer's salary.

She knew that just one month of income match wasn't enough evidence to quit her job. But in January, her

"

In my heart I wanted to take the leap, but I was terrified.

Because what if I take the leap and I fail?

blog income exceeded her lawyer's salary. Then it happened again in February. It was working.

Tanya got excited. She was ready to quit her job.

But no one else was; it's hard to ignore the comments from people you love:

"Are you sure?"

"Why don't you just keep doing both?"

"What about health insurance?"

"You're a state employee only two years away from the loan forgiveness program, just wait another two years!"

But Tanya's heart said something else.

> **I wanted to be happy now, not two years from now.**
>
> **In my heart I wanted to take the leap, but I was terrified.**
>
> **Because what if I take the leap and I fail?**

Tanya didn't quit her job. She had trouble sleeping.

For four months she kept going back and forth.

Then one day her daughter's tutor Brianne came over to the house with a navy and orange book called *I Am A Blogger.*

"I have a present for you," Brianne said.

"What is it?"

"My husband donated to this Kickstarter and they sent him two copies of this book. I don't know why, but here you go."

Tanya asks me to wait a second while she runs upstairs to get the book. She wants to show me the page that changed her life.

She comes back down the wooden steps with the blue and orange book, and tells me more about the day she first got it.

> **I'm literally freaking out over whether I should take the leap or not and whether I'm worth it. And I open this book and I see all these bloggers who took the leap, and then I read this paragraph in the first few pages:**
>
> **"We hope you enjoy reading these sixteen stories as much as we've enjoyed telling them. But more than anything, we hope when you close the back cover of this book you walk away with one very clear message: you are every bit as capable, worthy, and ready to take the leap as the people in this book.**
>
> **Will you?"**

Tanya took picture of that paragraph the first time she read it and texted it to a friend along with the following:

> **I'm quitting my job.**

She sent in her resignation letter and has been a full-time blogger since April 2019—less than a year since she made that pact with herself.

The comments from well-meaning friends and family didn't stop, even after she took the leap.

She tried to explain to some how much money her blog was making, but they worried she wouldn't make that forever. Her response?

> *It might disappear tomorrow, but would you feel any differently if I told you I was leaving to go start my own law firm? My own law firm wouldn't be a guarantee of consistent money every single month either.*

While even Tanya's lawyer-logic couldn't convince everyone, she realized she didn't need to convince anyone. Now it was time to simply go all in.

> *I just had to ignore the chatter and just say, I've made it this far and the only way I'm going to take it to the next level is if I put 100% into it, not just the 20% that I was doing.*

The day she quit her job wasn't easy-breezy, though.

> *I was a hot mess. But I'm glad I took the leap. And I don't even know why I freaked out that much because I'm still a lawyer. If things don't work out I can just go back to work.*

When you make big leaps, it's easy to feel like you're setting everything you built before on fire. But that's not true. It's still there. You can always come back if you want to. People forget that.

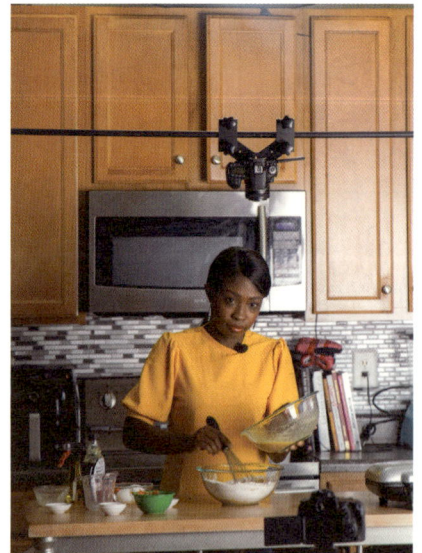

People still reach out to Tanya offering her legal work to do on the side. But for now, she kindly replies with, "No thank you."

"A LOT OF HER FRIENDS ARE ON YOUR EMAIL LIST."

Since Tanya quit her job, her blog continues to exceed her lawyer's salary month after month. How?

When she first started blogging she tried to do "all the things" and got quickly overwhelmed. She didn't really start making progress until she focused on just a few things, and she still focuses on those few things today: SEO, email, and content strategy.

Tanya makes only two kinds of content:

1. Recipes I'm excited about.
2. Recipes my audience is excited about.

While every recipe that excites Tanya doesn't always go viral or excite her audience, it's her most important starting point; if she isn't excited about it then there's little chance her audience will be.

But how does she know ahead of time what her audience might get excited about?

1. Google analytics.
2. A 99-year-old grandma.

BUSINESS BY THE NUMBERS

10,291 → EMAIL LIST SUBSCRIBERS

518K → MONTHLY PAGE VIEWS

REVENUE BREAKDOWN

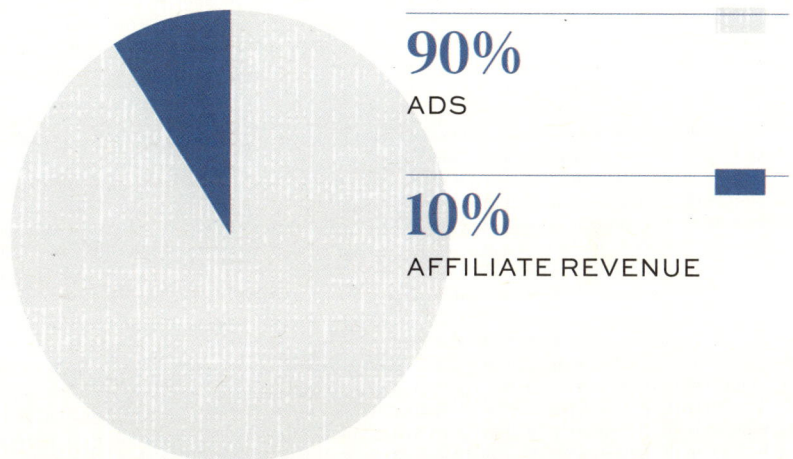

90%
ADS

10%
AFFILIATE REVENUE

Tanya analyzes her top posts on her blog each week and looks at Google Trends, but never writes about a trend she isn't also genuinely excited about. She makes most of her content decisions by pairing data with instinct.

Tanya also prioritizes qualitative data, like the time her husband took her oxtail meal to his grandma's house and she said: "This is the best oxtail I've ever eaten!" Since she's been on the planet for 99 years, Tanya knew that recipe would be blog-worthy.

Finally, Tanya looks to her email list for inspiration, which really started to take off when she created her first sequence—an air fryer email course (an idea she got from a podcast). She pays special attention to which emails get the most opens, clicks, and replies.

Today she emails her list at least twice a week: "I don't want them to forget me." She also segments her list based on their interests. There's an air fryer group and a pressure cooker group. She loves only sending affiliate products to people who might actually be interested instead of blasting her whole list.

To date, her email list is an intentionally dedicated group of 9,000 food lovers and growing. Unlike most websites (and conventional advice), opting into Tanya's list isn't that easy to find—and that's on purpose. Most of her opt-ins are at the end of relevant blog content; Tanya wants a more invested reader.

For now, she likes knowing that the people she's writing to on her list have actually read at least one full blog post. She loves knowing that she's only writing to people who actually like her content and *want* to hear from her.

Recently, Tanya's husband came home from the grocery store and said:

"This lady at the checkout said she heard of your blog."

Tanya responded: "No, she didn't. You're full of it."

"No. She said you're the one that does air fryer recipes. A lot of her friends are on your email list."

"THIS IS WHAT I SIGNED UP FOR."

But as anyone building a fanbase knows, the haters are never too far behind.

Tanya laughs as she remembers how she never got any negative comments when no one read her blog. But once it started to make a difference in people's lives and kitchens, the trolls came out to play too. This is hard enough for even those with the toughest of skin, but it's even harder for those who struggle with imposter syndrome.

Weak is not a word you'd use to describe Tanya. She's self-reliant. A former track athlete. A lawyer. Practical. But all the logic in the world doesn't keep imposter syndrome away when a rude comment comes in.

It always stings; even celebrities who've been in the public eye for decades confirm that. But what helps them keep going is what they choose to do after. Tanya's strategy?

1. Accept imposter syndrome as a fact of life.
2. Check the comments of your heroes.

When I ask Tanya about her biggest struggle, she talks about imposter syndrome. "I always feel like whatever I do, maybe it's not good enough."

When Tanya gets a negative comment her first instinct is to help. *Is there something she could have done better? Does this recipe need tweaking? Is there anything she can do to help this person?*

If the answer to all of the above is a clear "no," then the comment is moved into the "troll" category—labeled unnecessary and cruel.

Next, she goes to the website of a food blogger she admires. (Her two favorites are The Pioneer Woman, because she didn't go to culinary school, and Martha Stewart, who, according to Tanya, gets tons of unwarranted nasty comments on *really* great recipes.)

Every single time Tanya gets a negative comment, she reads a negative

> ## "
> ## This isn't happening because I'm not good enough, but because I am reaching more people!

one on Martha's blog. Every time. (I asked her twice just to be sure.)

Tanya flips the narrative—instead of the negative comment serving as evidence that she's not enough, it becomes evidence that she's on the right track, becoming like her heroes.

> *It reminds me that this is what I signed up for, and that a negative comment doesn't mean you're not making good recipes.*
>
> *When I put my first catfish post up, I didn't get any negative comments. It took me a while before I got my first "one-star-you-suck" comment. This isn't happening because I'm not good enough, but because I am reaching more people!*

For Tanya it's about ratios.

> *If I was getting more negative comments than positive comments, then I would self-reflect. But that's not the case. I'm getting more positive feedback.*

No matter what you do, you could put forth your best effort—it's not always going to make everyone love you. But that doesn't make you not qualified to do it.

When she's feeling down, she also likes to read all the positive email replies she's saved to remind herself why she's doing this in the first place. "It reminds me that you're not an imposter. You helped Jane in Colorado provide a wonderful meal for her family."

"BECAUSE I CAN."

And now it's time for me to watch Tanya cook.

The peaches have defrosted.

And the rest of the menu? Her air fryer steak and seafood salad.

Her daughter skips into the kitchen to help—she chops herbs as I mix them into the butter with minced garlic as a topper for the steak.

The whole cooking experience is calm and comforting.

In between the sound of chopping and Tanya's daughter's infectious laughter, I ask Tanya questions about how pressure cookers work and what you can do with an air fryer. (Days later when I leave Charlotte and return home to San Diego I find myself cooking big meals more often, relishing in the mess, and taking my time. Finding that same comfort in my own kitchen across the county.)

After about an hour or so of chopping and talking and cooking we all sit down to eat on a summer Tuesday at 2 p.m.

The garlic-herb butter melts on the steak, and it's the first time I've ever enjoyed a home-cooked steak without steak sauce. We don't talk much because the food is so good. I go back for seconds on the seafood salad and mentally plan to make it in my own kitchen as soon as possible (which I do). We all swoon over the peach cobbler—I don't even need the ice cream.

Before I leave, I ask Tanya about how her life is different now than it was last summer when she made her declaration.

It's generally assumed that when you quit your job your life becomes perfect, but of course, that's not the case.

Tanya didn't just quit a job—she got a new one, and that comes with a transition period. She's in that now. She's still trying to find the schedule that works best for her and is getting used to the idea that she's the one who's supposed to make it now.

The biggest change is what happens when she wakes up not feeling physically or mentally well. In the past, she'd have to go to work anyway. But now, she'll make new micro declarations, like "'I'm not doing anything this morning.' For me that's been the biggest reward so far." This example is fresh in her mind, because

it happened just the day before our interview.

Tanya woke up feeling down, incapable, and unmotivated to work on the blog.

> *One of the negatives you face being an entrepreneur is that you're always thinking about your business.*

Tanya was overloaded, and her mind and body were shutting down.

Instead of fighting it and pushing through, Tanya used her newfound freedom to take a break and go out to lunch with her husband (a filmmaker who also works from home and helps with her YouTube channel).

> *We said of course we would still talk business over lunch. But we didn't. We talked about basketball. We talked about random stuff. It was really relaxing to get away.*

Then she talks about the errands they ran together after lunch as if reading from a spa menu:

> *We went to the library. We got new books. We didn't listen to podcasts; we listened to music. Then we picked up our daughter, and went to the store. I didn't check Facebook, Instagram, or any of that stuff. I needed that. It was refreshing to not think about the blog.*

I don't even know where my suits are.

Tanya doesn't miss practicing law, but she does miss having a work routine and is in the process of applying one to what she does now. The reason she's struggling? "I'm in the kitchen to work. But it doesn't feel like work. It's weird."

The biggest change of all? "I don't even know where my suits are."

Tanya had to wear suits every day and follow other unspoken appearance rules. "As a lawyer you can't wear big earrings," she says animatedly as two green wooden earrings that almost look like cucumbers sway back and forth, brushing her shoulders. I take in the rest of her appearance as if I'm writing for Vogue: hair loosely pulled back with a scrunchie, tan cotton T-shirt featuring a smiling Tupac, stretch jeans, and fuzzy gray slippers.

While Tanya loves wearing what she wants, spending more time with her kids in the summer, and having the flexibility to take spontaneous family trips, that's not really why she's doing this.

One of the first emails I remember getting was from a guy who made my Instant Pot Jamacian jerk chicken soup; he wrote: "Thank you so much for that soup. I really wanted to impress my wife with the dish. She just loved it, and I really appreciate you helping me impress my wife."

Tanya talks about helping this man impress his wife at least three times during our interview, the email memorized by heart, her eyes shining as if she's talking about winning a Michelin star.

That's my goal. That's what I want to do. I want people to impress other people with this food. It just made me happy.

And then there's the woman with epilepsy who had always been afraid of cooking because what if she had a seizure and burned the house down? She emailed Tanya to say thank you for teaching her that air fryers had an automatic safety shut off; for the first time in her life she was cooking with joy instead of fear.

Tanya's blog started out as a place of her own, but what kept her going was people like this.

They also inspire her to keep challenging herself, like creating new spins on old recipes, which is risky; people don't always like it when she veers from tradition.

Sometimes I push a limit with something like a southern staple and people comment, "You can't do that. How dare you?"

Tanya's response?

Because I can. I can do that. ◼

The empty nesters

When the illusion of security leaves you
feeling trapped, how do you break free?
Find out how author coaches Steve and Azul
turned down big career advances, packed their
life into two suitcases, and found their freedom.

Steve felt trapped.

On the outside, his life looked great; he was an industrial engineer at the top of his career, managing a huge team and a multimillion-dollar budget for building a new hospital—something he'd always dreamed about.

But somewhere along the way, he'd lost that sense of imagination.

Why did he feel so trapped in a life he'd created, a life he'd worked for, a life he'd always wanted?

He wasn't sure. But he did start to wonder when exactly did he stop feeling free?

That question always reminded him of the maps he loved as a kid. He loved looking at big open maps—he'd always see them in 3-D, imagining the mountains and the waters, hoping one day he'd visit all those places.

"I was a sandbox kid," he tells me, a way to describe his free-flowing imagination; when he was young, the world was his sandbox.

But somewhere along the way, he'd lost that sense of imagination.

He wanted it back.

He started the way a sandbox kid might. With a glue stick.

Specifically, he made a vision mandala, a collage process he describes as "not like shopping in a catalog for more toys and more things or more stuff," but instead a way to begin to dream about a "way of living," to take a pause and ask yourself questions like, *Who do I want to be? How do I want to live? How do I want to be? What are my real dreams?*

On his first vision mandala, he glued pictures of things he'd dreamed about while staring at maps as a kid: The Eiffel Tower, Hong Kong.

He showed the finished product to his now-husband Azul, telling him: "For some reason, I think we're supposed to be living around the world."

Azul, a successful school principal, thought it sounded exciting. But they both knew it wasn't something they could act on right away. "We were raising two teenagers," Steve explains, "Azul's biological kids (I'm a bonus dad); we lived a regular life."

This wasn't the season for a drastic change, but they decided that now *was* the time to start planting seeds for their dream future.

And for them, the most important step in the early days was giving themselves the permission to dream at all, making it okay to question where they were and to dare to want more.

Steve and Azul didn't start thinking about how to finance their dream right away.

Money and business ideas weren't the driving force to their inkling for change.

"Revenue was the thing we had," Azul explains, "but we didn't have time. We didn't have connection. We didn't have what we wanted most: freedom."

But could such freedom really be possible at this phase in their life, deeply entrenched in successful careers and responsible for a household and two kids? "We weren't young like everyone else," Steve says. "We weren't millennials."

Could they really change their lives?

"I'VE GOT TO GET OFF THAT BRIDGE."

But they kept dreaming anyway.

They also kept working, Steve commuting an hour each way to his job (albeit in a nice convertible).

But material things just weren't important to him.

Steve kept making vision mandalas, and one day he cut out a picture of a man standing in the middle of a high bridge over dark grey water.

The man looked stuck there, in the middle of the bridge, and even though the man was clearly above the water, the look on his face made it seem like he was drowning.

Steve remembers staring at that picture and just knowing: "I've got to get off that bridge. I need to get across."

At that same time, he was offered a promotion and a $30,000 raise.

> ## " Now *was* the time to start planting seeds for their dream future.

He turned it down.

After talking it all over with Azul, they decided it was time for Steve to take the leap.

They would still be able to support the kids on Azul's salary and Steve would look for other jobs.

He got his real estate license, traveled by himself when he could, and dedicated most of his time to being there for their kids. And to make ends meet, Steve drove for ride-share companies.

He loved it.

Steve went from six-figures and first-class business trips to $12 an hour, and he was never happier. He loved making playlists, offering water and mints, and making sure everyone had the best possible experience. He felt like he was getting to create again, like his car was his new sandbox: "I lit up like a light bulb."

He no longer felt like he was drowning.

But they knew they couldn't sustain on $12 an hour forever. Buoyed by the momentum from Steve leaving

" Why not start now?

his job—the veritable proof that they weren't too old to make (and survive) drastic changes—they started to dream even bigger.

What if they could start their own business, perhaps one that would give them the freedom to travel the world one day?

"THIS SEEMS SORT OF SCAMMY."

Azul had always longed to be a creator and joined Steve right away in learning about business with the hope that one day—perhaps when the kids graduated—they might have a successful business together.

They weren't in a hurry. The kids were still in high school; health insurance was still a top priority. But they knew that starting and growing a business takes time, so why not start now?

They knew they wanted to travel, so an online business sounded like a good idea. They started following people who seemed to be experts on the subject.

They tried whatever the experts suggested. But as Azul noticed, "Some things didn't work. Even when certain online experts said, *Do this. We promise it works.* They didn't always work."

They became discouraged.

"This seems sort of scammy," they started to think about all they were learning from online business gurus. "We were both turned off," Azul says.

But then they found Pat Flynn.

And Chris Guillebeau.

And Chris Ducker.

Everything changed when they found the creators who resonated with them, who showed them that the internet was just another place to serve people and reach people, and that you could add real value online without being scammy or unethical.

Azul and Steve signed up for "all their email lists," so when Pat Flynn and Chris Ducker announced, via email, a one-day business mastermind in San Diego, where Steve and Azul lived, Azul signed up right away.

The event was a month away, and it would change everything, but not in the way he expected.

"IT TOOK ME 24 YEARS AND 30 DAYS."

The event would be in mastermind format, where each person goes into a "hot seat" to share their business and solicit help from the group.

Azul signed up because he was so eager to learn from Pat Flynn in person, but he had no idea what he would have to talk about when it would be his turn in the "hot seat."

Azul was still working full-time as a principal; he was terrified of being in the hot seat with nothing to say. But he still had a month until that would happen.

What could he create in the next month?

He'd always dreamed of writing a book.

> *I'd been studying and taking courses and reading books and talking about writing a book for years, but I hadn't done it. I decided, "You know what? I'm going to finally write that book."*

He wrote the book in 30 days and submitted it to an editor the day before the mastermind event.

> *I'd wanted to write a book for 24 years. It took me 24 years and 30 days.*

When it was his turn to be in the hot seat, he talked about his book. He also shared his story: his past business failures (a failed gym), his big dreams, and his sincere questions about how to become a creator.

But no matter what else he talked about, people kept circling back to the same thing:

> *Wait—you wrote a book in 30 days? And with a full-time job and family? How? Can you teach me to do that too?*

As a professional educator, Azul knew exactly how to teach what he'd done. So at that mastermind,

Steve was still driving, using his real estate license, and attending every one of their kids' track meets.

Their top priority was still, as Azul puts it, to care for the kids and "keep the nest going," all the while learning about business on the side, hoping one day—far into the future—they could achieve their travel dreams.

So it was quite the surprise to all of them when Azul was offered an opportunity to move to China.

"I COULD SEE HIS EYES LIGHT UP WHEN HE WAS DOING COACHING."

When their son was about to graduate and their daughter a junior in high school, Azul got offered a job to be an instructional coach in Shanghai.

But he was conflicted.

He was *loving* his coaching business, and at that time, all the coaching sessions were done in person in San Diego. How could he leave?

But then Steve showed him that first vision mandala and reminded him that China had been on it.

Azul had forgotten.

Steve also reminded him that they'd wanted to start an online business anyway—why not start coaching clients over Skype?

But would the new job even allow Azul to run a business on the side? Committed to his budding business,

he accepted his first coaching clients—one of them being Pat Flynn himself—even before he had any idea of what to charge; all from joining an email list and signing up for an event long before he was "ready."

Soon Azul started helping people write the books they'd been longing to write, while still working as a principal.

Azul decided he would only take the job if they'd allow him to continue coaching. He wouldn't accept the job offer unless they agreed.

And they did.

But there was still one more person to check with.

Their daughter.

"I asked her," Azul remembers, "Do you really want to go through your senior year in China?"

She did.

Their "nest" was also about to become even more secure—the new job, Azul shares, "paid for all of our housing, our healthcare, for schooling. It took a lot of pressure off."

There was just one last problem.

Although Steve and Azul were legally married in the U.S. on May 19, 2015, China did not recognize their marriage.

Steve shares:

> *I couldn't have a visa to go with him because China wouldn't recognize me as his spouse. The options I was given were to either find a job in China that would sponsor my own visa or stay in China for less than 60 days at a time as a tourist.*

For the first year, Steve got on a plane every 55 days and left China for Hong Kong.

Azul worked at the largest international school in China and did his author coaching on the side.

"I could see his eyes light up when he was doing coaching," Steve remembers, wanting to keep looking for ways for Azul to have the freedom to do that even more.

Steve started looking up online course creation tools like Teachable and brainstorming with Azul how to combine his teaching, coaching, and writing skills with Steve's years of leadership development experience in the corporate world.

In the evenings, they implemented everything they'd been learning over the years and built their first online course.

Then, Steve found a job in China so he wouldn't have to keep leaving. He got his own visa and managed operations for a large private elite international school in Shanghai.

For the next year, they both worked their full-time jobs in the day and worked on their online business at night.

It started to take a toll, despite all the perks that came with their jobs. Azul remembers:

> *We knew the symptoms of getting into something we knew we weren't meant for. It was so comfortable. They pay for your housing. They fly you back and forth to the U.S. We had a maid. We had a cook. We started to see*

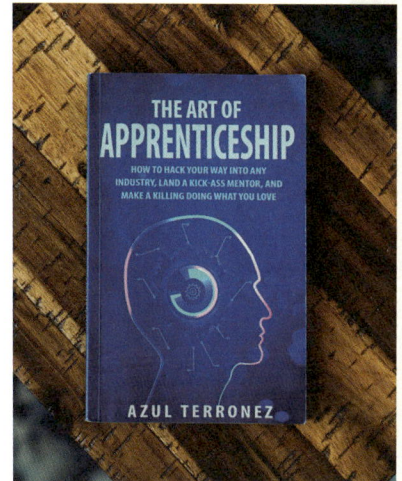

"

We started to feel
it shift when we
went all in.
You can't just sit
on your hands.
You have to keep
learning and
trying and testing
and failing.

how we could get sucked into this really nice lifestyle.

Then, because of his stellar work performance, Azul got offered an even more lucrative job—a director role in Brazil. This time, the offer also included a visa for Steve and assistance in finding him a new job in Brazil.

But when Azul told Steve about the new Brazil opportunity, Steve's first thought was about the way Azul's eyes lit up when he was coaching. Azul remembers exactly what Steve said to him that day:

I don't think we'll grow our business if we go into the traditional job route. We have to escape.

Azul wasn't so sure.

"LET'S NOT BE BOUGHT BY SOMEBODY ELSE."

Meanwhile, the team recruiting for the Brazil job finished drawing up their very lucrative offer and presented it to Azul. It was time to make a decision.

Steve's eyes water as he tells me what he told Azul that day:

I don't want to do it, Azul. I love the travel, but let's do it our way. Let's not be bought by somebody else. I don't want to be bought out.

Steve remembers the fear he felt then: how intense of a risk he knew they'd be taking, and what it felt like

to have his heart's desire in direct conflict with security.

It was like we had to let go of security again, and I had already let go of it when I took the first leap. I knew—it's not fun sometimes, eating rice and beans. I just didn't want to be poor. I didn't want to give up an income or have him sacrifice such a beautiful opportunity on paper.

But Azul turned down the job.

He, too, wanted something more than "beautiful on paper."

They wanted beautiful in real life.

They wanted to *create* something beautiful themselves.

Not only did they turn down the Brazil job, but with both kids now off at college, they both quit their jobs in China to go all in on their business.

And as far as security, Azul knew that the skills they had weren't going anywhere.

We could always return to our careers; we're really good at them. But we have to give this business a shot

Azul, who recently turned 50, remembers how confused the people around them were when they told them about their decision.

When you're closer to the end of your life, you start to get less risky; our friends and family thought

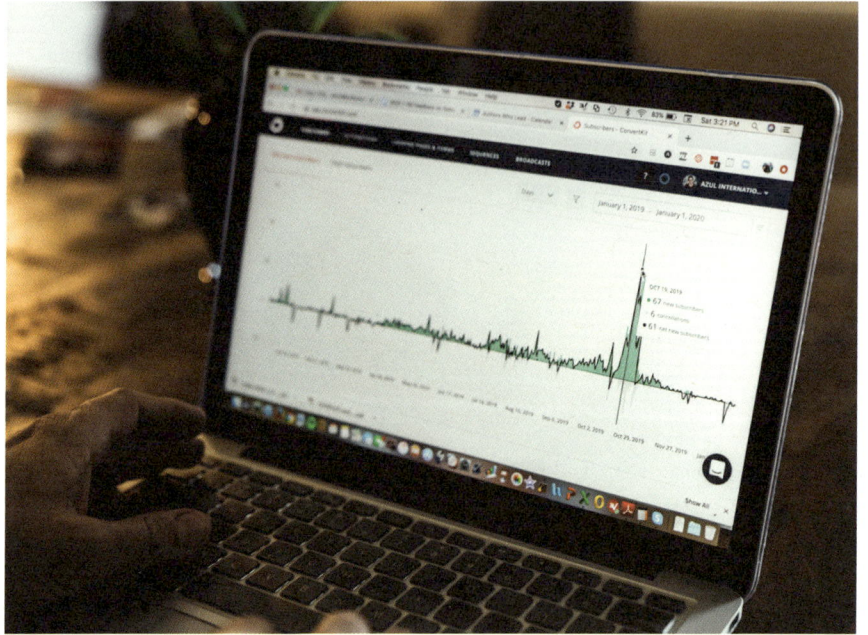

we're crazy and probably still do, but man, what a joyous choice.

They sold or gave away everything they had. "We put our life into two suitcases each," Steve recalls.

They traveled the world as cheaply as they could, keeping their living expenses as low as possible, and investing everything they could into their business.

"You have to invest money yourself and start to learn and take courses," says Azul. "Some work, some don't. We started investing in things that we hadn't invested in—like email, our website."

The investments paid off. Azul shares:

We started to feel it shift when we went all in. You can't just sit on your hands. You have to keep learning and trying and testing and failing. If you don't fail, you're going to get stagnant. You have to try things and stay focused.

They learned and tried and failed every day, with all their hearts, with all their focus.

They learned something new every day, and some things, they had to hear over and over before they finally clicked. "We were resistant for so long to email," Azul remembers.

I was just afraid: What do I say? But as we started to grow our email list, we realized people want to hear from us. They want to know what's going on. They want to know about our podcasts and about the programs we offer.

Azul says he's not afraid anymore:

Now email is a big part of our business because we realize we're leaving a lot of revenue off the table if we're not communicating with our people who really want to hear from us.

For Steve, email is "part of my new sandbox, where I go in and play."

"THE SECURITY YOU SEEK IS INSIDE OF YOU."

Steve and Azul quit their jobs and left China to go all in on the author coaching business in 2017.

Two years later, their business income exceeded the combined income they made in their previous lucrative careers.

Since then, the business has continued to grow and evolve, and today it exists as *Authors Who Lead*, a perfect combination of the skills they've both developed in their decades-long careers: "We help leaders write and publish books people love," Steve says.

Learning online business was just a means to an end, a way to help them bring the expertise they already had to the proverbial online table.

Azul also started a podcast called *Authors Who Lead*, and Steve has one

BUSINESS BY THE NUMBERS

2,000+ → EMAIL LIST SUBSCRIBERS

50+ → BOOKS PUBLISHED

200+ → AUTHORS HELPED

REVENUE BREAKDOWN

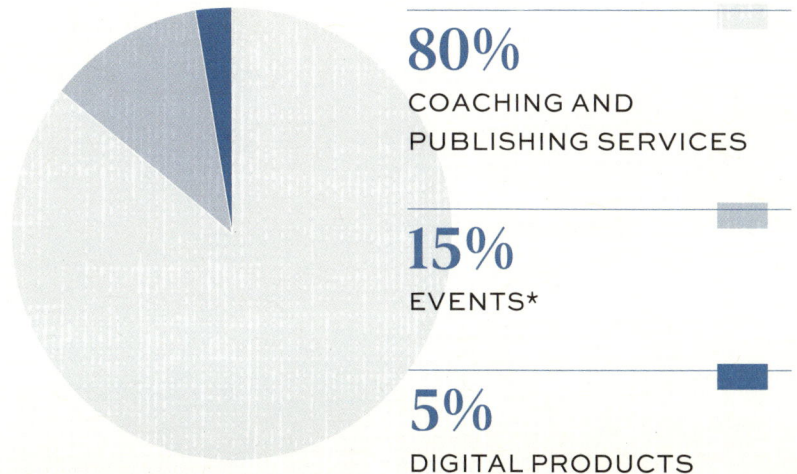

80%
COACHING AND PUBLISHING SERVICES

15%
EVENTS*

5%
DIGITAL PRODUCTS

(including in-person and online: mastermind, summit and workshops)

called *Soul and Stories*, "for people who feel stuck."

Because Steve doesn't feel stuck anymore.

Recently, it was a big dream come true for him to take his parents to Europe—they'd never been overseas.

And when Steve's dad was diagnosed with a terminal illness, Steve was able to take a pause from the business to become his dad's patient advocate. "What a lovely gift. I could step out of our business because of the lifestyle we created."

They are so thankful they gave themselves permission to dream years ago, when most would have told them they were "too old" or too far along in their careers to dream of anything different.

And it's not always about rushing to quit your job or changing everything tomorrow.

For Steve and Azul, what mattered most was the slow, dreamy, open permission to "set a new intention for a new pathway," and being open to whatever happens next, without needing to know "all the answers."

A kind of return to childhood, as Azul explains:

> *When you started out in life, you didn't know what would happen—and we still don't. It's just we think we know what will happen. We think we have security. It's all an illusion. When you take a leap, you're going to want security from things, but the security you seek is inside of you.* ■

The five-month runway

What happens when you give up traditional expectations to fund your biggest dreams? Find out how Teela from *Every Tuesday* went from crying during her commute to covering her family's living expenses for a year with one launch.

Sometimes, Teela cried during the hour-long commute to her agency job as a graphic designer in Atlanta.

Her job was to help create visuals for brands.

But she wondered if she was enough.

Her superiors kept rejecting her designs, and it made her question her worth as an artist.

> *Am I just not a good artist? Should I be pursuing something else? Nobody wants to use the artwork I'm making.*

Maybe she'd chosen the wrong career?

But there was only one problem.

She couldn't stop making art.

And she couldn't turn off her desire to share it.

So she started focusing her attention on making art in the evenings, and instead of looking for affirmation at work, she shared her art online.

People *loved* her work, and their positive reception changed her outlook. "I have something to offer," she started to believe for the first time, a crucial realization for any artist.

And while that didn't completely stop the tears on her commute, they transformed into a kind of liquid courage. Instead of crying in resignation, she'd ask herself bold questions, brainstorming ways to stop the tears; maybe she should look for another job?

Or maybe, just maybe, it's time to build her dream business?

Teela dreamt of having her own business since her first job out of college, where she worked for an early-stage startup. The chaos she saw there empowered her:

> *I realized, it's okay if you don't have it all figured out. You can still have a business and figure it out as you go.*

She was determined to figure out how to turn her art into a business that would allow her to quit her job.

"WHEN I GOT HOME FROM THE DAY JOB, THAT'S WHEN MY LIFE HAPPENED."

When Teela was in first grade, a friend asked her what she wanted to be when she grew up. Her answer was instant: "An artist."

She asked for art kits every year for her birthday, and she'll never forget her parents' reaction when she'd show them something she created: "Oh, you're a great artist," they'd say.

She didn't know what it meant to be a professional artist then, but she knew it's what she wanted to do, and she believed that somehow, she'd figure it out.

So when she started to feel artistically unfulfilled in her day job, she created a blog as a way to share more of her art. She'd started blogs in the

> It's okay if you don't have it all figured out. You can still have a business and figure it out as you go.

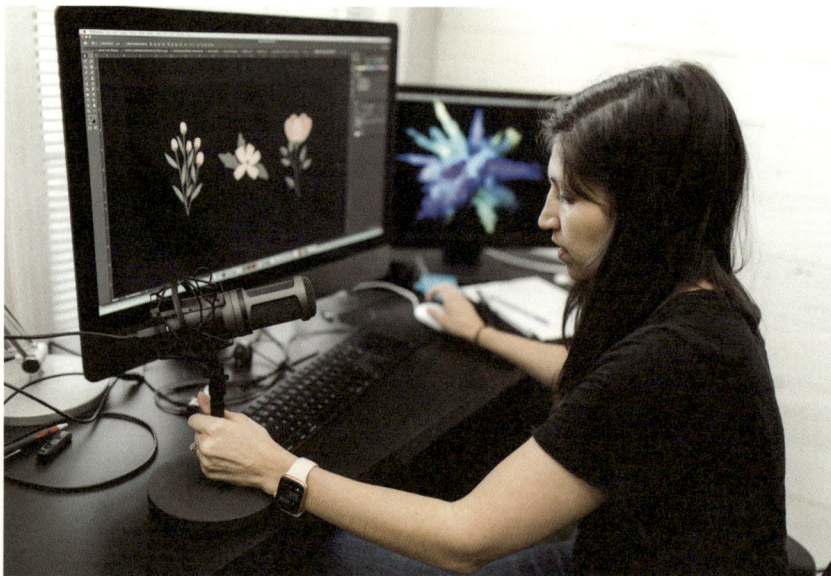

Teela had no idea yet how to turn this thing she loved into a job, but she was determined, and she had that thing you can't rush—momentum. By this time, she'd created something new every week for almost two years.

Teela followed several bloggers and YouTubers who made a full-time living with their work, but she had no idea how they were making money. But because of them, she knew that it was possible.

She wasn't crazy.

She began with trial and error—putting herself and her art out there wherever she could, keeping her eyes wide open for any opportunity to share and teach, add trying out new platforms as she heard about them.

Her original strategy was to try everything, hoping something would stick.

So when she heard about this new free online design tool called Canva, she submitted her designs. When she heard about a new platform called Skillshare, she created and sold her first online course on letterpress printing.

That's when she made her first $600.

It felt like a million dollars.

past but struggled to be consistent, so she decided to call this one *Every Tuesday*, in hopes to dedicate herself to her craft every week, each Tuesday.

She started Every-Tuesday.com in October 2013 and shared her art along with written tutorials so others could create every Tuesday along with her.

Then, that Christmas, her fiancé bought her a USB microphone, and in January 2014, she shot her first YouTube video using the mic and sharing her screen.

She found it was more natural for her to teach using video. She kept going, sharing a new video every Tuesday, often staying up until after midnight to create.

She didn't make any money with it. But she loved it.

It felt like hope: *If she could make $600 doing something she had already been doing for free for almost two years, what else could be possible?*

The momentum was starting to pay off, and it gave her the energy boost she needed to direct her attention toward figuring out how to build from that $600 and learn how to make a sustainable full-time living with her art.

"LET'S SEE HOW FAR WE CAN GO."

She kept making new courses on Skillshare, and every time she did, her income grew.

In addition to those courses, she also created and sold hand-lettering fonts.

Through years of content creation and lots of trial and error, Teela's business model was born: creating digital art products and teaching others how to create digital art products.

Getting in on some of those trends, such as hand lettering, really helped her build momentum in the early days, but what helped her turn that luck into a *sustainable* business, was:

1. Creating *a lot*.
2. Paying attention.

In addition to creating constantly, Teela also put just as much attention into noticing how people were responding, especially paying attention to what questions they asked and what they requested more of.

She listened intently and let her audience inform what she created next.

Her business was built on a feedback loop: create, listen, create, listen, create, create, create.

But despite the new income coming in, her business wasn't consistently matching the income of her day job. It was, however, requiring more and more of her time to keep up the pace of creation that was working so well.

She started to feel the tension, and she wasn't sure how much longer she could continue staying up after midnight to keep her business afloat.

She also had other things to tend to that year—2015 - like planning her September wedding.

When she wasn't creating for *Every Tuesday*, working at her day job, or commuting, she was looking for a caterer, a DJ, and a dress. They'd been saving money for a year to pay for everything.

As the wedding day grew closer, *Every Tuesday* continued to accelerate, until one day, momentum took over and not only did it begin to consistently match Teela's income, but it looked like it might also match her fiance's as well (he also worked at the same design agency and sometimes helped her with *Every Tuesday*).

They were both unhappy at their day job.

They couldn't help but wonder: what would happen to their growing business if they both went all in?

It would be risky for both of them to quit at the same time, but they knew they could always go back and get an agency job. This business was growing, and it felt like now was the time to see what it could really be.

But the income wasn't super consistent yet. They would need some financial runway to feel comfortable enough to quit their jobs.

They remembered all the money they'd saved for the wedding.

Quitting their jobs sounded better than a wedding.

So instead of having a big wedding in September 2015, Teela and her husband got married at a courthouse and quit their jobs to go all in on *Every Tuesday*.

Their wedding money would give them five months of financial runway to see if they could make this work. If it didn't, their plan was for her husband to go find a job.

But for the next five months, they vowed:

> *We're in this together. Let's see how far we can go.*

"THAT'S SOMETHING THEY JUST DON'T TEACH YOU IN ART SCHOOL."

They were still absolutely terrified.

They'd said goodbye to stable income.

They had five months of living expenses.

Teela directed all her energy toward doing more of what was working, but now at an even faster pace with full-time dedication and her husband as a full partner.

She kept listening and kept creating—one of her videos on watercolor even went viral (it has over 3 million views to date).

YouTube became a place where she would beta-test her course ideas. If a video did really well, it was a good sign that it might be a great foundation for a course.

As she created more courses based on what videos were doing well, her income grew even more.

But what really changed everything for her, she says, was giving as much time and attention to learning online marketing as she did to her learning her craft.

I definitely invested a lot of my time into learning online marketing. I knew just being an artist and putting out really beautiful artwork wasn't going to be enough to keep my business running long-term. I knew that if I wanted to push my business to the next level I needed to learn online marketing, because that's something they just don't teach you in art school.

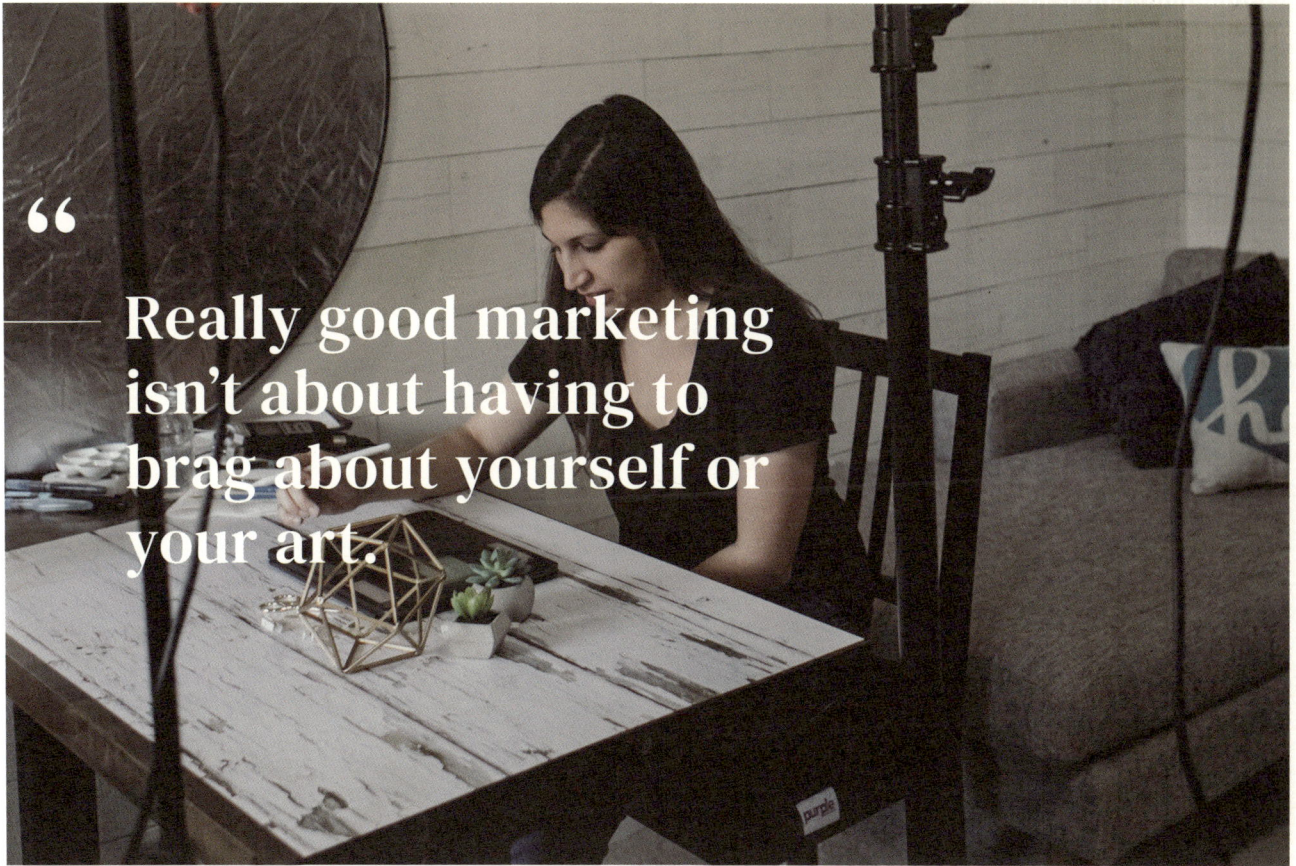

> ❝
> ── **Really good marketing isn't about having to brag about yourself or your art.**

Easier said than done, especially for artists, so I ask Teela what helped her get comfortable with marketing as an artist.

For her, it was finally understanding that really good marketing isn't about having to brag about yourself or your art; it's actually the opposite.

Good marketing is about understanding how your craft will serve someone else and then sharing your creative work as an act of service, making it all about your audience, not about you.

That was freeing.

To learn online marketing, Teela listened to podcasts, like *Smart Passive Income* by Pat Flynn.

She'll never forget hearing Pat say, "If I could do it over again, I would've started my email list sooner. That's the biggest thing I would've changed."

Teela started her email list right after hearing that episode.

But she was still scared.

your imagination (or fear, for that matter) tricked you.

It's not a stadium, at least not now.

It's more like your living room: a few of your closest friends on the couch, snacks on the side-table.

Teela wrote her emails honestly, telling her small but growing email list:

> *I have no idea what I'm doing, so I'm going to try and figure it out, and hopefully you'll be along for the ride.*

She started slowly, writing two emails a month.

> *I didn't want to inundate people with too many emails. I didn't want to discourage them from staying on my list. And I was secretly scared that if I started emailing them every single week I would lose a bunch of people.*

But Teela's business name—*Every Tuesday*—kept nudging her to email weekly. Finally, she realized:

> *I'm Every Tuesday. It's okay to hear from me every Tuesday. And if they don't want to hear from me every Tuesday, then why are they following me? It doesn't make sense for us to maintain this relationship if you don't want to hear from me every Tuesday.*

While a few people dropped off, her list kept growing (people joined her list via the free resources she'd share on her YouTube tutorials).

"I HAVE NO IDEA WHAT I'M DOING."

Teela knew that to do email well, just as when she started *Every Tuesday*, she'd need to be consistent so that they'd remember her.

But that's when that new-platform-fear kicked in. That moment you're about to share your work in a new space and, even though you're just beginning, you somehow feel like you're about to walk on stage in front of a stadium full of people to give a speech without having anything prepared.

It's terrifying.

But creators like Teela do terrifying things every day (or at least every Tuesday).

And the best part is, when you walk onto that new "stage," you realize

And instead of her email list being "annoyed" that she emailed them each week, she got email replies like this:

> *Teela, I don't know if you're going to get this, but I just wanted you to know that I look forward to every single Tuesday now because of you.*

Email, Teela says, was the key to the next phase of her business; she loved YouTube and Skillshare, but she didn't own her audiences there. Email gave her the ability to bring them from those platforms onto her own, opening the doors for the course launch that would change everything.

"OKAY. WE CAN DO THIS."

Now that she had her own audience to communicate with directly, she felt ready to create longer, more in-depth, self-hosted courses.

Her first two self-hosted courses made five figures each.

Teela realized that people were willing to pay even more for a course that had more in-depth teaching. And self-hosted courses seemed like a great pillar for her business model—if they could have consistent five-figure launches, they could really keep this going.

Her third self-hosted course focused on teaching people how to convert their handwriting into sellable fonts.

BUSINESS BY THE NUMBERS

41,000 → EMAIL LIST SUBSCRIBERS

239,000 → YOUTUBE SUBSCRIBERS

270+ → VIDEOS CREATED

14.5M → YOUTUBE VIEWS

1.8M → EMAILS SENT

100,000 → STUDENTS TAUGHT ONLINE

REVENUE BREAKDOWN

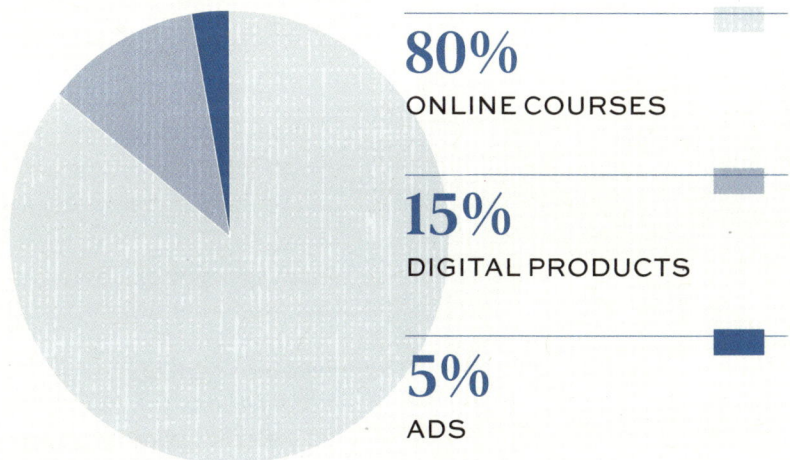

80%
ONLINE COURSES

15%
DIGITAL PRODUCTS

5%
ADS

By this time, she'd been building an email list for two years and had created about 12 courses prior.

She launched her third self-hosted course in March 2017, hoping for another five-figure launch.

But that didn't happen.

It made six figures in its first week.

That one launch covered their living expenses for the next year.

It was the first moment they truly felt like they could breathe, the first moment, *two years after quitting their jobs*, where they firmly, finally, felt like, "Okay. We can do this."

"I WISH I HAD KNOWN THAT BACK THEN."

Sometimes, Teela can't even believe that this is her life—she still vividly remembers what it felt like to cry on the way to work.

I ask her what advice she has for any creators who are there now, creatively unfulfilled in their day job, in pain, and perhaps also questioning their worth as an artist:

Whatever people are saying or thinking about your work at your day job, whatever is making you miserable, that's not your worth. However people make you feel, that is not your worth as an artist.

Your worth comes from how you feel about yourself when you're creating the artwork that you want to create for yourself. Stay focused on your aesthetic, the goals that you have, not the goals that other people have for you wherever you're working.

Stay true to yourself and stay focused on your own goals because that's what's going to carry you. I wish I had known that back then. I wish someone had just said that to me because I questioned myself so many times.

And it's really, really important to remember why you started this to begin with. I mean, you had a love for art, you had a passion for it at some point, find that passion again. Do it for yourself.

Teela and her husband still work on *Every Tuesday* full-time. They even paid off all their debt—their house and all their student loans.

Do they regret trading a wedding for a business?

In a word?

No.

Or even better, the answer can also be found in a name.

Last year, they had their first child. A baby girl.

Her name?

Tuesday. ∎

Getting comfortable with instability

Unexpected twins would change anyone's life. But for parenting blogger Nina Garcia those babies pushed her to turn her $200-a-month–earning blog into a full-time career reaching lonely moms everywhere.

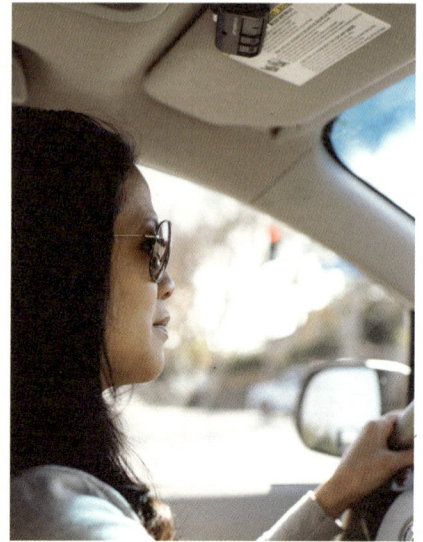

When Nina Garcia found out she was expecting her first child, she bought all the books and signed up for all the classes. But, as she remembers it, "there's a difference between knowing it in your head and actually experiencing it."

She went into labor in the middle of the night, and from that moment on, nothing was quite like what she expected.

No matter how much she prepared, and no matter how much she deeply loved and was grateful for her beautiful son, parenthood was still a shock to the system. She was thrown. "I miss my old life," she thought. "Will this ever get better?"

She didn't really know.

Like most intense changes in our lives, it doesn't matter that millions or even billions have experienced them before—what is also universal is that in those first moments we often feel utterly and completely alone.

But then, while searching for answers in the middle of the night, Nina discovered blogs and forums where moms were sharing their honest experiences.

She *wasn't* alone.

She decided to become part of the conversation too.

On March 4, 2010, she started her own blog, sleepingshouldbeeasy.com. The name was inspired by sleep-deprived musings she and her husband shared about the irony that something as natural as sleep could cause so much turmoil in their lives.

You'd think that something like sleeping—something that comes so naturally and is such a necessary

<blockquote>
There's a difference between knowing it in your head and actually experiencing it.
</blockquote>

part of your day—would be easy. You would think that babies would just fall asleep, but of course it's not the case. That was sort of the irony of it. I was like, "It should be easy." But of course it's not in the beginning.

She blogged weekly for years, with no intention of it ever becoming more than a way to build community and maybe help another mom out there feel less alone.

Then she got news from a doctor that would change everything.

"WE'RE FINE WITH ONE."

Nina and her husband both came from big families, so when they decided to start a family they hoped to eventually have four kids.

But after their first son was born, Nina changed her mind. "I think I'm good with one," she told her husband.

One sounded good.

But when their son was almost three years old, the inkling to have just *one*

more rose up for Nina. They'd try for just one more, a sibling for their son.

They were thrilled when she got pregnant.

At the first sonogram, the doctor came in to tell Nina some news.

She was not going to have one baby.

She was going to have two.

The Instagram version of this story would include feelings of being hashtag blessed and grateful, and those feelings would come in spades for Nina—she knew what a brutal journey many go through just to conceive one child in their lifetime.

But if only the sufferings of others tempered our own in the moment; life just doesn't work that way, and I'm honored that Nina shares with me the truth of what she felt when she first found out—the kind of truth you usually only hear behind closed doors, sitting on living room rugs with your best friends.

"I was devastated," she tells me honestly. "That first week, I cried every day."

She was overwhelmed with questions.

How will my body take to carrying two babies?

How will we afford two babies?

She thought about all they had gone through with their first and couldn't fathom doubling that.

And when she started googling "twin pregnancy bellies" she became even more terrified of what was to come.

"I literally threw my phone across the room," she remembers.

In those early days, she was consumed with one daunting question:

How am I going to do this?

"MY ULTIMATE DREAM WAS TO EARN $200 A MONTH."

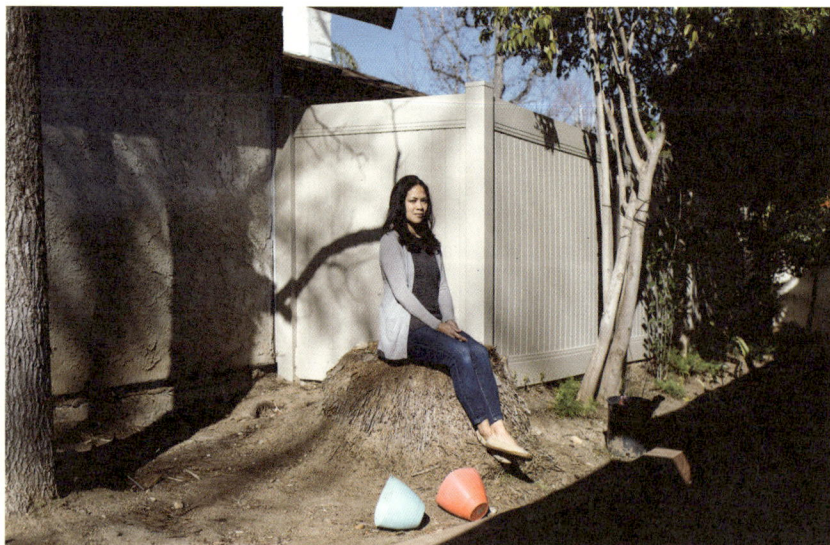

With the help of friends, family, forums, and blogs, Nina got through it. She had two healthy twin boys and was grateful for her family of five.

But money was *tight*.

All the income from her day job in graphic design was going toward childcare.

As her kids got older, she longed to do things like take them to the zoo, but they couldn't afford it.

Then she remembered her blog.

At this point she'd been blogging for five years and had made some sporadic money from ads.

She knew some people made a full-time living from their blogs; maybe she could find a way to make just enough money to take her kids to the zoo and do other fun things?

My ultimate dream was to earn $200 a month.

So for a year, while raising her kids and working a full-time job, Nina dedicated her nights and weekends to building her blog.

She never felt burnt out; she loved it.

If I was at home, then I would be working on the blog. I guess you just find the time if it's something that's really important to you.

For me, that was willingly saying no to a lot of things that frankly

> " **I guess you just find the time if it's something that's really important to you.**

were not even that interesting. But I'm a homebody. I love being on the computer and writing and doing all the quirky website stuff. It was a source of joy for me.

Between ads and a company that reached out to have her do a sponsored post on infant cushions to help babies sleep better, she felt like she'd reached her "ultimate dream," making almost $200 in her first month (to this day she still remembers the exact amount: $197.52).

A few months later, with the goal of learning more about how to make consistent income with her blog, she invested in what was then a new online course called *Elite Blog Academy*. Nina remembers how the very act of paying for the course shifted her mindset.

I'm invested in this; I'm going to put everything I have into it.

She applied everything she learned from the course, focused

> ## It almost felt like if I worried enough about it, then at least I wouldn't be disappointed if something bad did happen. I was trying to beat worry to the punch.

on increasing her traffic through Google, Pinterest, and SEO, and kept writing about her experience being a mom of three.

There was also something the instructor of the course, Ruth Soukup, said in April 2015 that stuck with Nina:

> *"Imagine if you could quit your job a year from now."*

Nina never planned to quit her job.

But then, as the year went on, her mom—who helped out a lot with the kids and childcare—got sick and had to be hospitalized.

Nina felt like she constantly had to ask for time off work to pick up her kids from school, and she started to feel the strain.

She hated having to ask for someone else's permission to take care of her kids.

Ruth had planted a seed that Nina's job frustrations began to water, and

she couldn't help but start to dream an impossible dream:

> *What if I could quit my job?*

"THOSE FIRST FEW MONTHS WERE SO TINGED WITH FEAR."

Nina worked even harder on her blog, using all her spare time and implementing all the strategies she was learning.

A year after buying the course, her income grew steadily, and was close to matching her full-time income, but not quite. She just needed a little more time.

At that same time, her childcare costs rose so high that she wondered if it might make more financial sense to quit her job now to take care of her kids and work on the blog.

Six years after starting her blog, and one year and one month after Ruth

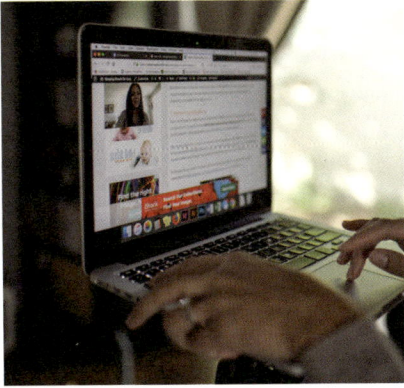

27,000 → EMAIL LIST SUBSCRIBERS

38% → AVERAGE OPEN RATE

inspired her to dream bigger, Nina quit her job.

She couldn't wait to see what would happen with her blog when she went *all* in, working on it as her full-time job.

It was indeed a dream come true.

It was also a bit of a nightmare.

"Those first few months were so tinged with fear," she remembers. With her predictable income gone, the steady paycheck was swiftly replaced with steady worry.

> *It almost felt like if I worried enough about it, then at least I wouldn't be disappointed if something bad did happen. I was trying to beat worry to the punch.*

To stifle the constant barrage of worry, she took freelance jobs from her former employer to supplement the income gap between her blog income and her old paycheck.

REVENUE BREAKDOWN

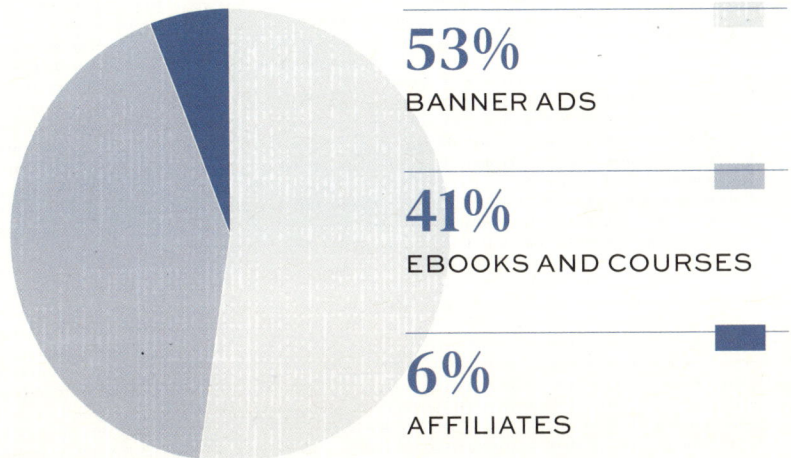

53%
BANNER ADS

41%
EBOOKS AND COURSES

6%
AFFILIATES

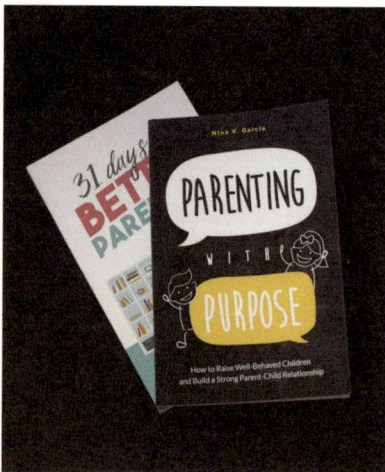

The freelance work helped silence her worry for a while, but after five months of freelancing, she realized her blog had stalled.

She hadn't grown her blog income by even one penny despite working on the blog "full-time" for months; she was still earning the same amount she'd been earning when she worked on it part-time.

> *The whole point of leaving the job was so that I would increase the blog's income now that I had more time for it.*

She'd really wanted to see what would happen when she gave it her all, but she was struggling to get there. First worry took over—and now, freelancing.

She was disappointed in herself.

She'd love to say she got bold and decided to take the big risk and say no to freelancing and yes to going all in on her blog—but being responsible for three kids is no joke. The true story is that there was no big leap, no big revelation.

The freelance work just dried up.

And she'd be lying if she said she wasn't terrified when it did.

But the month she lost her freelancing work was also the month her blog income finally jumped.

Each month, it increased.

Sometimes it decreases, too. But Nina started to shift her interpretation of the instability that had paralyzed her when she first started—she realized the instability was not a reflection on her, her worth, or even her blog's potential.

Once she realized that there will never be this "I made it; I'm never going to have to worry again" feeling, the worry dissipated.

And the more the fear faded, the more her income grew.

> *When you're always operating from that fear mindset, you're inhibited. You're not able to think creatively about what you can offer, how you can change your business, or how you can grow your business.*
>
> *You're always turning to the past like, "Oh, I wish I had the stability of that paycheck," rather than thinking creatively; "Okay, well how can I turn this business or this blog into something that makes my salary or more?"*

She realized that the only way she was going to make this work was to accept the fact that if she wanted freedom, she also needed to get comfortable with instability.

> *It's always going to be unstable. That's just the essence of being an entrepreneur. It's not going to be consistent paychecks every month.*

But, rather than seeing it as a source of fear, I try to see it now with excitement and faith.

"A LOT OF THE TIMES PEOPLE BUY FROM YOU AFTER THEY'VE KNOWN YOU."

With renewed commitment, Nina went all in, and in April 2017 she replaced her full-time salary.

She did that primarily through making her own products, like ebooks and courses, and selling them through her email list, which she says helped a ton when her blog traffic started to dip due to changing search algorithms.

Because I constantly run sales on my digital products to my email list every month, I didn't suffer the effects of it as drastically as I would without it.

It's not a coincidence that the Mondays I send my newsletters out are also my highest traffic days.

If she wanted freedom, she also needed to get comfortable with instability.

Now she's even working on turning her most popular email newsletters into an ebook.

> *One of my favorite things to do is writing my weekly newsletters; you're not beholden to Google Search terms or what's popular. I see it as more like the personal side of me. I'm able to just share advice and insights that probably won't make for good SEO, but it really touches lives and impacts people.*

And that personal relationship Nina builds with her audience is also what helps her sell her products. "A lot of the times people buy from you after they've known you, after they've had several emails from you."

But what she loves most is getting the email replies like this:

> *"Wow, you read my mind. How did you know? Every time I open your email, it's exactly what I'm going through."*

Nina's work helps moms feel less alone.

And no matter the instability or what may come next, she's thankful she took the leap, because in addition to the freedom and income, it gave her something precious—five words she now carries wherever she goes, an immutable fact:

> *Oh, I can do this.* ∎

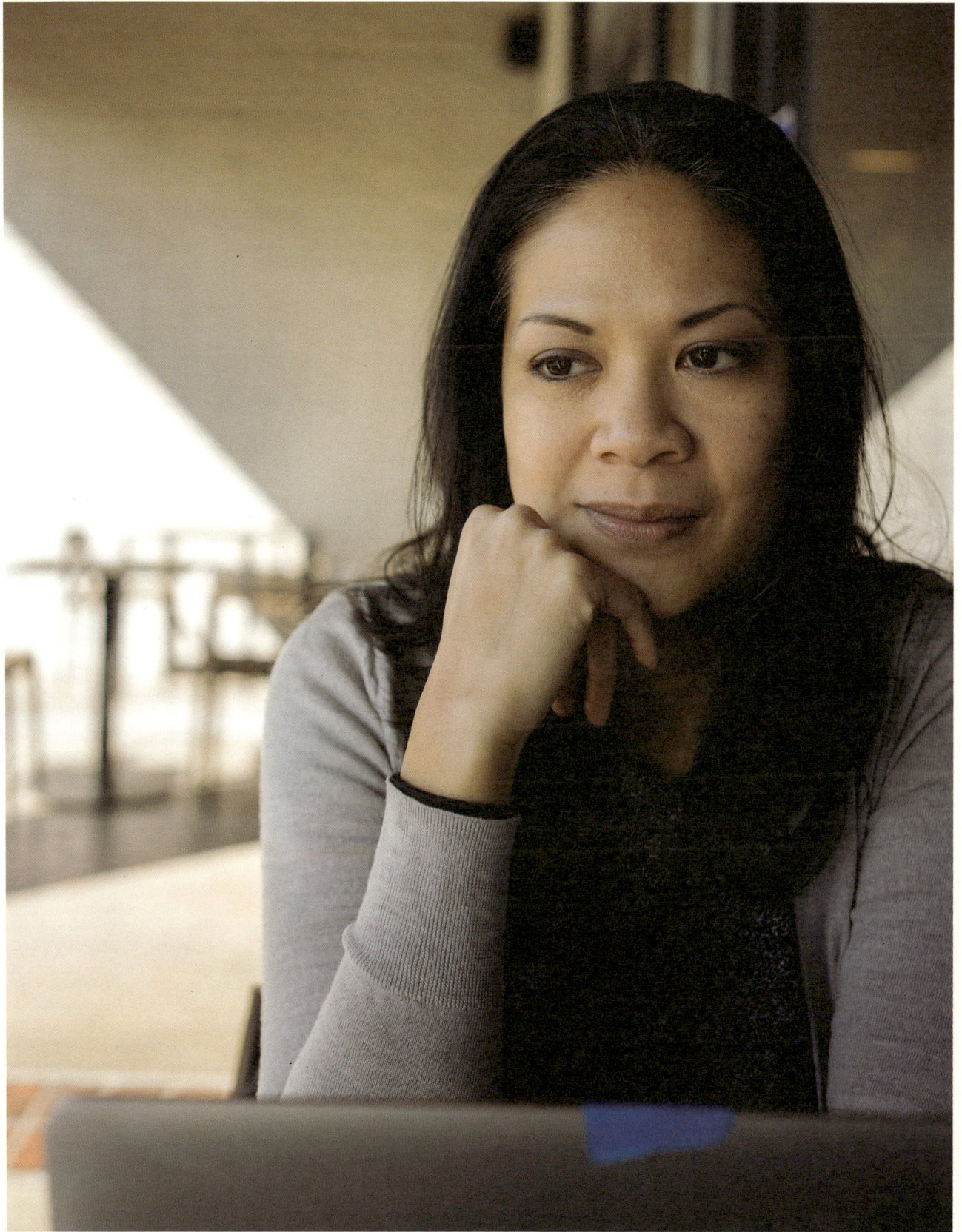

CHAPTER THREE

Never giving up

THE CREATOR JOURNEY IS HARD.

For every stroke of luck or opportunity, there are a dozen valleys where you're tempted to give up.

A lot of advice out there says when it gets hard you should just push through—push, push, push. Exhausted? Oh well. That's what it takes. Go harder. Sleep less. Don't stop.

But one size doesn't fit all when it comes to persistence.

And while burnout might be a way to create one thing—it's not a sustainable way to be a creator.

These stories are about what creators did to keep creating even when tragedy struck, when fear or critique threatened to squelch their voice, or when having kids slowed down (but didn't stop) their creative output.

"Never giving up" looks different for everyone, and taking time to do the important things in life—like grieve or have kids or rebuild a life after everything falls apart—is worth it. Your creativity isn't going anywhere. It actually thrives in the valleys and the pauses, even when we can't see it.

Giving up isn't always a bad thing.

But giving up on you—on your creativity—is.

Because no matter what obstacles you face, it's you and your creativity that will help you keep going.

Fireproof optimism

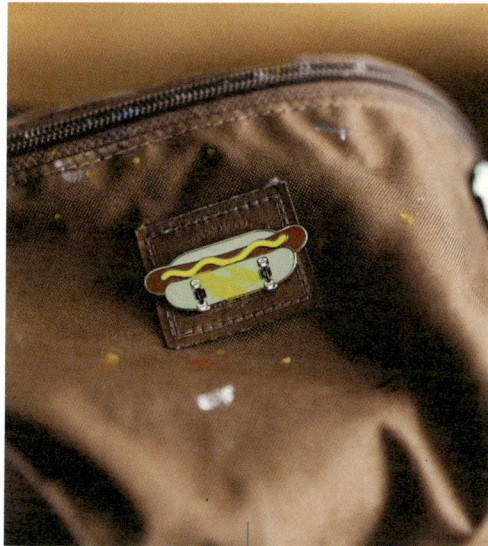

Faced with devastating news, many would crumble
under the weight of life–altering circumstances.
But when muralist Eric Friedensohn lost everything
in a fire, one charred message left behind
reminded him he could choose his idealism.

Eric doesn't usually create in the early morning; his best work typically happens at night.

But on this particular morning, he got up earlier than usual to paint a sign for his friend's tattoo shop. He opened all the windows of his second-floor apartment that day.

He smelled something weird, but brushed it off. This was New York, after all. Things smelled weird sometimes.

He closed the window closest to him to keep out the smell.

But it kept getting stronger.

And stronger.

It smelled like burning rubber.

He got up and walked to the window again to see if he could find out where it might be coming from, and that's when he saw that the entire alleyway that made up his "backyard" was completly engulfed in flames.

And they were rising toward his apartment.

His whole body went into panic mode. Flooded with adrenaline, he went into accelerated autopilot, driven to survive.

His first instinct was to close every window to protect himself further from the rising flames; he burnt his hands on the now-piping-hot windowsills.

Then, the last window he closed exploded all over his face.

He heard more glass bursting. One by one, every single window exploded, shards thrust into his apartment like confetti.

Everything inside of him told him to run.

Get *out*.

But what about Pocket? His cat. He looked everywhere for those gray and white stripes, the pink nose, but she was nowhere to be found.

He had no choice but to get out of there as fast as he could, leaving his cat, his sign, and all his art, behind. There wasn't even time to put on shoes.

He ran.

He got out.

He stood on a New York City street in socks.

And waited.

The fire department came and put out the fire and assured Eric not to worry, his apartment would just have some smoke damage; his stuff, his art, his cat would all be fine.

Two hours later, once the fire was out, Eric and his then-girlfriend (who came as soon as Eric told her about the fire) went back into the building to look for their cats (she had one too).

They couldn't believe what they saw.

Everything was black, charred, reduced.

The mattress was just a small chunk of foam rolling on the boxspring.

And as Eric remembers it, "the ceiling was on the floor."

In two hours, they'd lost everything.

In two hours, they were homeless in New York City.

Also, their cats were gone.

Before they turned to walk out and find a place to sleep for the night, Eric noticed that the scanner he used to save his sketches still looked almost intact, aside from the fact that it was melted shut.

Something compelled him to pry it open.

Inside was one of the only things that survived the fire, a small scratched lettering sketch he'd done earlier that week and had forgotten about.

The letters spelled just one word.

"Optimist."

"OPTIMISM ISN'T THE SAME AS HAPPINESS."

The sketch survived, but it was damp, fragile; it could disintegrate easily. No one would have blamed Eric for letting it fall apart, leaving it there, renouncing optimism for a while.

But he did something else.

He paused, right in the middle of the char, with firemen in the background saying they needed to leave the place immediately—it wasn't safe. But Eric stood, holding the only thing he had

> **And while he lost the art in his apartment... he was still an artist.**

left, and remembered who he was two hours ago.

He remembered what he was thinking when he created that optimist sketch: that he was an optimist. And he could still choose to be one.

"Optimism isn't the same as happiness," Eric shares. It isn't the same as life always working out or believing that people get what they deserve or that everything happens for a reason or always works out for the best. (He's the first to talk about all the privileges he's had in his life, especially compared to the injustices and suffering he's seen firsthand in his travels for art projects around the world.)

But he decided optimism could be a choice—you could *feel* pessimistic and still *choose* optimism.

The most powerful optimism is the kind that still stands after a fire, even if it's fragile, even if it's still grieving.

What binds all true optimists together—wherever they fall on the spectrum of wealth and power and privilege—is a single belief:

I can get through difficult things.

And in that moment, holding that soaked, barely-holding-on sketch, Eric knew he was going to be okay.

He also knew that he wanted to do more with his life.

If he had slept in that day, hadn't woken up early to do art, he likely would not have made it out alive.

He started questioning everything:

If I did die tomorrow or today, am I happy doing what I'm doing right now? Or am I waiting for something on the horizon that might make me happy?

Though he was now without a home, any of his physical belongings, and without his cat, the optimist sketch reminded him to think about all he still *did* have, like his life.

He'd made it out alive. That alone made him incredibly grateful.

He also still had his family—his brother even created a GoFundMe campaign to help after the fire—and he had his health.

And while he lost the art in his apartment—sketchbooks, art supplies,

> "
>
> ___
>
> The most powerful optimism is the kind that still stands after a fire, even if it's fragile, even if it's still grieving.

I think that everybody starts creating art when they're a kid, and they are technically an artist because an artist is someone who creates art. But then at some point, they stop.

that sign he was painting for a client—he still was an artist.

He could make more art.

And that, when he really thought about it, was exactly how he wanted to spend whatever days he had left.

"I GUESS I JUST NEVER STOPPED."

One of Eric's greatest privileges was his grandma, Rita.

She was a stained glass artist who made a living doing work she loved, welding colored glass together by hand in her basement to make windows and lamps. (After she died, Eric was given one of her glass lamps. It's in his studio now, cracked in places, but he plans on restoring it soon.)

Grandma Rita bought Eric art supplies and art books, always encouraging him to keep his imagination alive.

He grew up with a unique and precious gift—the belief that doing work you love for a living was possible. In

fact, it never even occurred to him that you couldn't make a living in the arts.

I think that everybody starts creating art when they're a kid and they are technically an artist because an artist is someone who creates art. But then at some point, they stop. Because other things get in the way or they don't see it as a viable career option. I guess I just never stopped.

And as Eric got older, his love of making art grew.

By the time he was in high school, he knew he wanted to be a professional artist.

I felt the most alive when I was making something. I knew that was a pretty good sign you should do that for your career: if you feel really alive while doing something and there's also demand for it in the world. That's the sweet spot, right?

109

He went to school for graphic design and started doing paid projects as soon as he could, finding most of his clients on Craigslist. For his senior thesis, he did a project on the art of hand-painted signs, and ended up designing a sign for one of his favorite coffee shops. He loved how it felt to have his art on a wall, connected to a place, a community, he really cared about.

He also loved the freedom of having his own business, even during the times when things were slow and he'd have to take projects he didn't like or find temp work to pay the rent that month. He thrived on the adventure of it all—an artist in New York City. He was grateful for the privilege.

But when the fire happened, freelancing had to pause. He lost a lot of money in the fire, and he was mentally frazzled and burnt out from the trauma. He needed consistent income to help him find a new place to live and replace everything he lost.

He got a job at an agency that specialized in event design. He hoped the day job would be a great learning experience and a chance to make more connections.

It ended up being another opportunity for him to see his art on a larger scale—they produced designs that wrapped entire busses and served as huge backdrops for large industry events.

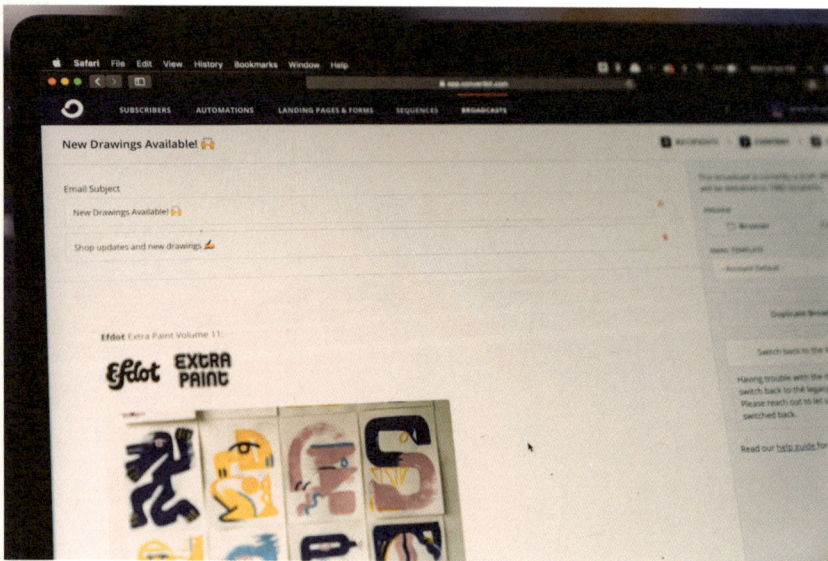

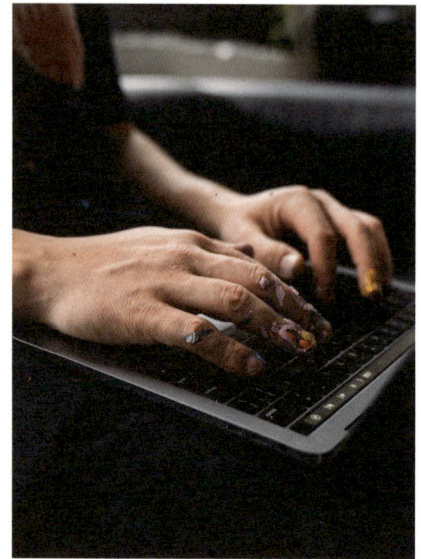

Eric saw his designs literally get bigger.

But then, thrown away.

> *A lot of this stuff would get thrown in the trash just a few days or weeks after I designed it because it was for events. Most temporary events lead to a lot of waste and I didn't like that. I just thought to myself, "How can I make large-scale art that's a little more permanent?"*

"THERE WAS NO CLIENT, THERE WAS NO ART DIRECTION. IT WAS JUST ME."

At the office, there was a big wall covered in chalkboard paint.

No one really used it.

One day, compelled to create, Eric stayed at work after hours to create a huge chalkboard mural lettering piece, just for fun. It was the first time he'd created something like that since the fire, since the optimist piece.

When everyone walked into the office that morning, they were floored. They loved it. It changed the whole feeling of the office that day, and Eric saw firsthand how art could bring people joy and change an environment in an instant.

It was also the first time he realized his *personal* work could impact others.

> *There was no client; there was no art direction. It was just me.*

Eric didn't know when, didn't know how, but he knew that he wanted to do more work like that—he wanted to get back to creating his own designs from his own vision, not someone else's.

A year and a half after the fire, he quit his job and decided to give freelancing another try. He traveled more, getting inspired by the world around him and channeling it all into large-scale pieces.

He was especially drawn to murals, their sense of permanence and community.

During this season, he also broke his leg skateboarding and endured multiple surgeries and intense physical therapy.

He couldn't walk unassisted for 14 months (and he lived in a fourth floor walkup apartment).

But it was just another setback that fueled his creativity.

Since he couldn't skateboard, he channeled his love for skateboarding into his designs. And people loved them.

Eric also had a lot more time to share his work online.

And while painting murals was difficult at this time too, he started using photoshop to design the murals he dreamed of painting when he could walk again, drawing over photos of real walls, hoping he could eventually use them as mockups to pitch to local businesses.

That's how WeWork found him.

They needed someone to paint murals at their locations around the world, and they reached out.

Eric was hesitant at first; he didn't want to go back to another day job, making art to meet someone else's vision.

But the more he got to know the people and the job description, the more he realized he would have a new kind of artistic freedom there.

It would also be a chance to do a lot of murals—his favorite.

He took the job.

And the artistic freedom wasn't a false promise. Eric's skateboarding hotdog design was turned into a neon sign for one WeWork location.

He worked there for three-and-a-half years and loved the experience painting things that felt more permanent. He also never stopped creating his own personal work and sharing it with his audience online.

That audience, and their support, he says, always gave him a sense of freedom—that whenever he was ready, he could still leave the day job and go back to freelancing.

Which he did.

He loved the WeWork job, but as happens to many hardworking creators in a day job, his work was recognized and he was promoted.

> # If there's one person out there who deeply resonated with something I made, that has to be enough for me.

But sometimes, moving up means getting further from the art and more into management.

Pretty soon, Eric was only doing art 20% of the time, managing others the other 80%. At the same time, he got an offer to do a big freelance project from someone who had been watching his work online.

That's when he knew it was time to move on.

"TRY TO BE A REGULAR HUMAN BEING."

Before the fire, Eric had been blogging and emailing weekly for years, sharing what he was learning about lettering, design, and New York City.

People loved getting the behind-the-scenes of his creative process and hearing the stories behind the art he was creating. He used his email newsletter to interact with people who liked his art, and they became some of the first people to buy his pieces directly.

He cares a lot about trying to reply to all the emails and comments he gets in return. His online audience-building strategy might be one of my favorites; he doesn't care much for the latest online marketing advice. His guiding light, his goal for everything he does online?

Try to be a regular human being.

Seems like something you wouldn't have to remind yourself of, but it's surprising how fast the "rules" and "advice" of the digital space can drown out your own voice, that special thing people are looking for more of online.

For Eric, being a regular human being means communicating online in a way that feels authentic to who he is. He enjoys sharing his process, sharing the stories behind his work. In his blogs and emails, he tells people exactly how he makes things, breaking it down step by step.

People love that. I think a lot of artists want to keep their secrets to themselves because they're

113

worried that other people will steal them and take their business away and do it for cheaper. But I do think there is enough work to go around and I don't like to think about it as competition.

He gets email replies like "I can't believe you're sharing all this. Thank you for showing up each week and spending the time to share the behind-the-scenes or to just tell a story that's worth telling."

Most people are surprised he even takes the time. But when he started emailing, it wasn't about sales for him.

I wasn't doing it to get their sales, I was doing it because I really wanted to share, and I think the internet is a great tool for finding other people who are into

the same thing you're into. I like making new friends. I think at that point, I was trying to make more friends.

Today Eric has his own business, Efdot Studio, getting commissioned to do murals, selling prints, and teaching art workshops (we even hired him to share his story on the main stage at ConvertKit's annual conference, Craft + Commerce). He's made a lot of friends.

If there's one person out there who deeply resonated with something I made, that has to be enough for me. I try to drive myself back to that because being able to see how many people liked and commented on every single thing, it's easy to forget about the deeper connection of it, not just the superficial number.

Like, did this actually resonate with anyone deeply? If I get one really deep comment or direct message, that just makes me feel really excited that I'm doing this for something bigger than myself, and that's really rewarding.

"OPTIMIST TIPS."

A few days ago, Eric got a text from a friend whose apartment had completely flooded. She asked him to give her some "optimist tips" as she called them, because she wasn't, at that moment, feeling very optimistic.

He pulls out his phone and reads me what he texted back:

I'm sorry to hear the news. I'm glad you're okay. Remind yourself of everything you still have and be grateful for it. You are an optimist. Good things happen to you and because of you. You are okay and it will be okay. It only gets better from here.

A few weeks after the fire, Eric got a call from his old building superintendent who lived atop the building that shared the alley where the fire started.

The super found Eric's cat, Pocket.

After the windows in Eric's apartment exploded, Pocket also decided to make a run—a jump—for it. She jumped over the fire, window-to-window, and escaped into the opposite building.

The super found her hiding beneath a couch, ash on her face, paws scorched. She had to be admitted to an animal hospital and given oxygen for a few days. But she was alive. And Eric was grateful to now count the optimist sketch as one of two things the fire didn't destroy that day.

Eric will never forget that kind of life audit—where you are forced to step back, literally and metaphorically shoeless, and remind yourself of all the good things you still have, how much worse it could have been.

And while after the fire he longed for murals, for that sense of permanence, he also came to appreciate the myth of permanence: even a mural could burn up, get torn down, graffitied.

Anything can disappear in an instant.

His goal now is to make the most of every instant that he does have, spending it in the ways that matter most to him, making beautiful things for people, just like Grandma Rita used to do. ■

The lifecycle of creativity

Setting an environment for art to thrive takes not
only a keen eye, but also a continual learner's heart.
Fine artist Kimberly Brooks takes on each
new technological shift as an opportunity to
communicate the things that never change.

Kimberly Brooks says she likes my outfit—dark high-waisted jeans, a Taylor Swift-Stella McCartney T-shirt with a kitten on the front, black wedge sneakers, and a red-striped blazer. On any day, from anyone, a compliment like this would make me smile—but when *Kimberly Brooks* compliments my style, I *glow*.

Kimberly knows a little more about fashion, color, and style than most. One of her early painting projects, *The Stylist Project*, was featured in *Vanity Fair*, *Vogue*, and internationally recognized around the world—a portrait series where she asked stylists to come out from the background, style themselves, and pose for a painting.

I feel silly that I can't remember what Kimberly was wearing that day. I was too distracted by her face—open, giving, framed by shoulder-length wavy-blonde hair—and, of course, her paintings.

Standing in her artist studio I find it hard to look away from the *Jerusalem* canvas, a piece from her latest body of work that is more architectural. It takes up the entire back wall, and I almost walk right through it as if I'm in some elevated version of *Blue's Clues*.

But instead of gushing about her art or herself, Kimberly is excited to show me the artist she just live-streamed an interview with today for her online course. She believes deeply in what she calls "giving artists oxygen," or sharing space so all artists can thrive, something she did on a grand scale with her First Person Artist weekly column, then going on to found the *Huffington Post* Arts section which she grew to 20 million views per month.

Kimberly has been making a living as an artist for a long time, embracing every digital transformation, seeing every technological shift as just another way to communicate the things that never change. But looking at Kimberly, you would never guess she's been blazing art and technology trails for decades. Her face radiates with open-heartedness, coupled with a pulsing, Yoda-like energy of someone who can tell you things that will change your life.

I sit across from Kimberly in the garden just outside her Southern California studio. The wind is strong, rustling the pages of my notebook filled with questions I barely glance at for the next hour. I can feel the space expanding, the oxygen growing.

Kimberly's eyes have a kind of directive about them, as if they're quietly willing you to be the artist you never thought you could be, giving you permission to be more than you ever thought possible.

And maybe that's because Kimberly knows what it feels like to hide your art, to run away from what you really want to be doing. And what it takes to finally become what you never thought you could be.

119

"THIS IS THE BEST RED MONEY CAN BUY."

You can be anything you want, just as long as you're a doctor first.

That's what Kimberly's parents would often say. She came from a family of doctors and "the thought of being an artist for a living was not an option. That was against the law. That was like going to Mars. It was not even remotely a possibility."

As a kid, Kimberly was always drawing and always insisted on redesigning the yearbooks at school. She loved color and painted with acrylic and watercolor—but for some reason, painting with oil felt sacred to her: "I felt like it was something you needed permission to do."

Her college dorm at UC Berkeley happened to be right next to a tiny art store, and after classes she'd go inside and stare at the colors. She was drawn to this one tube of oil paint: "Cadmium Red." She asked the store clerk about it, who explained, "This is the best red money can buy. It's brighter than a fire truck, redder than blood; it's the perfect red."

Kimberly bought it and kept the red tube in her book bag. But it remained unopened. "It took me years to muster up the courage to just paint in oil." But by the end of her senior year, she couldn't ignore it anymore.

She drew a pencil sketch on canvas and dipped her brush right into the tube (she laughs as she

> ❝
> # Kimberly knows what it feels like to hide your art, to run away from what you really want to be doing.

remembers how she had no idea what she was doing).

As she moved the brush through the air, dripping with that pure red, something began to change. The moment the red touched the canvas, she knew: "Oh. This is what I'm going to be doing the rest of my life."

She said it felt like someone had taken a razor blade to the parachute she'd been living under her entire life. It was scary, but she was drawn to that sliver of sky, determined to become an artist.

> *It's one thing to be considered "talented" and another to doggedly pursue being an artist. You need both.*

Kimberly graduated Valedictorian in English Literature and got a job as a speech writer. But it didn't take long until the ache to paint started to grow.

> *The job looked great on the outside, but I had to follow my calling. I think if you have an artist inside you, you know it.*

It's one thing to be considered 'talented' and another to doggedly pursue being an artist. You need both.

After a giant earthquake hit San Francisco, Kimberly knew it was time.

It was like two hands in the sky shook me and I thought, "I have to figure out how to paint for the rest of my life."

She moved to Paris to paint and made money playing piano in bars at night.

Paris was as romantic and inspiring as promised, but for her, being surrounded by all that older European art was strangely less inspiring to her than the world she left behind.

Instead of standing on the shoulders of giants, I felt their weight. I couldn't wait to get back to California.

Kimberly moved back to California, but Paris had its effect. She came back to the U.S. resolved to find an answer to one question:

How will I design my life so I can devote it to painting and being an artist?

"ART IS COMPRESSED TIME."

It took her years to figure it out, and it wasn't easy. But what she learned turned into her "ecosystem of creation"—the system she teaches in her online course *Oil Painting Fluency & Flow* One of her favorite things to teach is creativity as a lifecycle.

Too many artists make work and don't show it or don't take themselves seriously enough to produce a body of work.

In those early years, she dedicated herself to the system she would one day teach:

1. Make a body of work.
2. Take it (and yourself) seriously.
3. Share it with the world.

All three steps are essential for a professional artist. And all are easier said than done.

To make her body of work, she painted constantly, continuing even after her two kids were born, painting every night after she put them to bed, deliberate about making time to make art:

I definitely had to protect my space to create. Art is compressed time. So artists are always trying to maximize the amount of time they have to create.

She took creative day jobs in the early days that allowed her to both pay the bills and have time to paint.

She grew her artistic knowledge during this time as well, taking courses at an art school she'd one day teach at, learning all she could about her craft and the artists and painters that came before.

The internet didn't exist when Kimberly first shared her body of work, first discovered sequences—that you could schedule emails ahead of time to go out in a series—she impulsively created *The Narrative Painting Project* to share the stories behind her paintings.

Her list became another place to show up, share, and give oxygen. People love getting her emails, myself included—it feels like a small gallery experience in my inbox, a chance to catch a breath and see the day with a painter's eye.

"I KNEW SOMETHING WAS TERRIBLY WRONG."

Kimberly's first foray into teaching started when painting made her sick.

After more than a decade of painting, she noticed she started to feel funny from the smell of solvents—painters use solvents like turpentine to wipe off oil paint in between strokes.

> *On a fundamental level I knew that solvent exposure couldn't be good for anyone, but I didn't realize how harmful it was. It is so liberally encouraged in art schools and art stores.*

But one day she felt so sick she couldn't get out of bed for three days.

> *I knew something was terribly wrong, possibly unnatural, with the way I was painting and I wanted to learn more.*

but she did the things that always work, in any decade, with any technology: show up and show your work.

She showed up to galleries with her paintings and got her first show that way. And because she remained dedicated to her ecosystem—always creating, showing up, showing her work, learning—her paintings kept selling.

It wasn't long before the momentum and critical acclaim led her to becoming the contemporary artist and leader in her community that she is known for—having exhibitions, teaching workshops, and speaking at prestigious institutions around the country.

She started an email list because she wanted to have direct communication with the people who were interested in her work. When she

She took some time off to dive deep into the subject. She researched how oil painting methods have changed in the last few centuries, and she learned that solvents were not only unnecessary, but also were not a foundational part of original oil paintings at all.

She found a way to paint more naturally, without harmful chemicals and without getting sick.

She reached out to her alma mater, The Otis College of Art and Design, and started teaching painting classes so she could spread the word. She also wrote a book: *Oil Painting Safe Practices, Materials, & Supplies: The Essential Guide* (Chronicle Books).

Once she learned about online courses, it was a natural transition, the perfect way to reach more people with this vital information. A few months ago, she used her email list to launch her first course, *Oil Painting Fluency & Flow*, an eight-week comprehensive program that covers everything she's gathered from a lifetime of oil painting.

She put a lot of care and attention into building a course that would fill in the gaps she was seeing:

> *Painting instruction today is often quite idiosyncratic, involves harmful solvents, and skips some of the more technical aspects involving basic craft. I developed this curriculum that not only integrates all the secrets and fundamentals of*

BUSINESS BY THE NUMBERS

7,200 → EMAIL LIST SUBSCRIBERS

COURSE BREAKDOWN

8 WEEKS   **8** LIVE SESSIONS

80 VIDEOS   **4** LIVE STUDIO VISITS

62 ARTISTS   **0** SOLVENTS

REVENUE BREAKDOWN

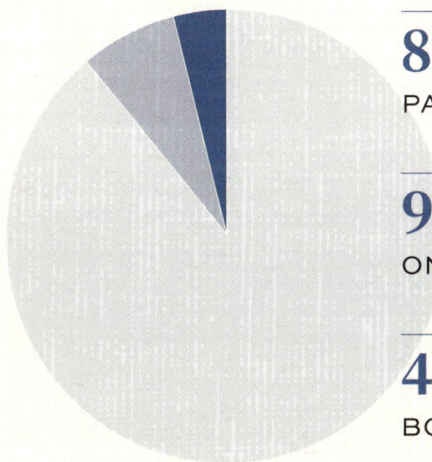

87%
PAINTINGS

9%
ONLINE COURSES

4%
BOOK SALES

And one of the weekly live streams she does for those students is starting in five minutes.

"SOMETIMES, MY PAINTINGS ARE LIKE MY PATIENTS."

Kimberly's assistant Heather arrives to help her prep for the livestream, and as we wrap up our conversation in the garden, Heather hands Kimberly a clipboard filled with thumbnails of paintings—the way a nurse might hand one to a doctor. And as if Kimberly knows exactly what I'm thinking, she turns the clipboard toward me and says, "Sometimes, my paintings are like my patients."

This clipboard is part of her ecosystem; it falls into the space between creating and taking your work seriously—it's the editing phase. These printed pages clipped tightly feature rows of small thumbnails of the paintings she's working on. At the top is a table of contents that reads:

Paintings in Progress...p.1

Rescue Missions...p. 4

Paint Over...p.9

how to build a painting, but also weaves in in-depth studio visits with other contemporary artists.

The course has been going so well that she's launching her first masterclass soon: *Build a Body of Work*.

To date, she's had 58 students from at least four continents—artists, writers, art professors, a Disney animator, a doctor, and even a tech CEO.

There are eight "Paintings in Progress." Below each thumbnail is a tiny typed caption noting where she left off or what she wants to do next. She keeps track of her editing process, a part of taking the work seriously; I can literally feel more oxygen enter

> # "Greatness is in the editing.

my lungs when I read it, the reminder I never tire of needing hitting me again, this time with a visual:

Greatness is in the editing.

Below the painting titled *Los Angeles* is the directive, "Flatten some sky. Lighten some leaves." Another, called *Green Room*, has a note written in pencil: "needs one side gilded."

Kimberly believes the key to creating art that resonates is to take the time—just like a doctor does—to *study*.

> *Studying craft inside and out, gaining fluency, is the key to finding your voice.*

Craft is what arms you with the tools you need to share your unique voice clearly, unmuddled.

It's this ecosystem—the editing, the boldness to create a body of work and showing up to share it again and again—that gives every artist the real chance at the dream of being seen and making a difference.

"Studying craft inside and out, gaining fluency, is the key to finding your voice.

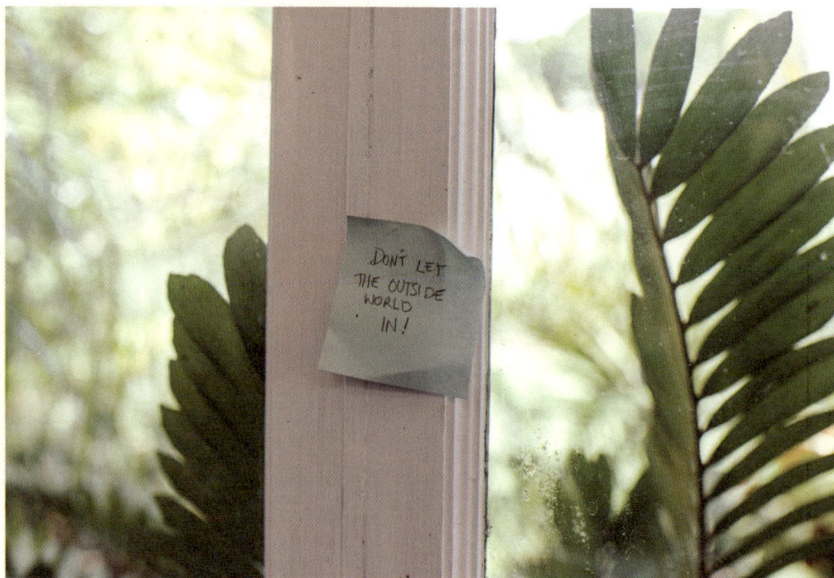

(A few weeks after our interview, Kimberly mails me a custom painted notebook as a gift. Grey and black hues swirl and jut up all around, with a fiery orange-red hue decidedly emerging through it all, strong, upwards. I almost cry when I smell the fresh paint, see the red.)

Today, Kimberly's art is prolific; she's been featured in numerous books internationally, published an essay that went viral called "The Creative Process in Eight Stages," gave a TED Talk on the same subject (which also inspired an album), and started a blog interviewing artists in their studios. Her paintings are still exhibited around the world.

Her breadth of accomplishments, high energy, and artistic self-assuredness can almost make you think she's fearless. But just before she clicks the red button to begin her live lesson she tells me that she's far far from fearless:

I've been afraid plenty of times. But I think I kind of like it. I get bored when I'm not a little bit afraid. ∎

Making friends with fear

For anyone pursuing a dream, fear will inevitably show up to distract. Motion designer Austin Saylor learned to accept fear not only as that unavoidable pain point, but also as a sign of his growing commitment and confidence in his work.

It was the middle of the night, and Austin shot up out of bed—someone was banging on doors in the nearby apartment breezeway. His wife Rachel bolted upright and asked, "Did you hear that?"

They listened closely. Someone was shouting.

> *Get out! Get out now!*

The banging was getting louder and louder.

They were scared and confused. What is going on?

Then Rachel saw smoke: "There's a fire," she breathed.

Austin opened the front door and saw "a wall of flames" just 10 feet from their door. He called out to Rachel quickly, "We're leaving now. Get the dog."

They grabbed their French Bulldog, Mr. Willoughby, two suitcases (already packed for a trip they were supposed to leave for the next day), and left, but not before waking up their nearby neighbors to make sure they got out safely too.

They lost everything else.

"The whole thing just burnt down to a crisp," Austin remembers.

It was a long time before Austin could sleep through the night again, traumatized that at any moment he and his family would have to leave—or worse—wouldn't wake up in time to escape.

"I could be dead," Austin remembers realizing later.

There were still so many dreams he wanted to pursue. And he was thankful he still had a choice.

Instead of sleeping in fear, waiting for the next bad thing to happen, he wanted to take back the reins, try to make good things happen.

He wanted to be less passive.

> *I'd rather be working really intentionally toward the life that I want rather than just hoping it happens one day.*

To start, he quit his graphic design job to pursue a longtime dream—animating and creating motion graphics. He planned to freelance just until he could find that next-step dream job at a studio that focused on motion

"I'd rather be working really intentionally toward the life that I want rather than just hoping it happens one day.

graphics. (He didn't believe he was good enough at animation to go out on his own yet, so he wanted to get more professional animation experience through a job.)

But that job would never come.

"WHY WAIT?"

Austin found his love for motion graphics later in his career. By the time he quit his job, he'd finished four intensive online courses on the subject, like Animation Bootcamp from School of Motion and Mograph Mentor classes.

He'd also been blogging about what he was learning in the animation world and sharing those learnings with his email list. Somewhere in the back of his mind he hoped to have his own business one day—but that felt like a very long way off. He started an email list without much of a plan.

> *I just knew I needed to have a list. I was getting one new subscriber a week for the first year, but I wasn't worried about numbers because I didn't even know what I was doing. I just wanted to build the practice of writing, publishing, writing, publishing, getting my thoughts out, and finding my voice through using it.*

He did find his voice, and a byproduct of finding that voice was that he also found a community—both via his email list and the groups he was a part of through those online courses.

After he quit his job, he let everyone in those communities know that he'd be freelancing, just until he found the kind of job he was looking for.

People started referring Austin for freelance work right away. He'd built up so much trust by being a contributor for years, never asking for anything in return.

He was shocked by all the work he was getting, especially since he considered himself such a beginner in the field. But he realized "the pool of freelancers is small and not everybody's available all of the time. A lot of people get too much work, and they would pass stuff to me." (He even did motion graphics work for ConvertKit.)

The freelance work kept coming.

And coming.

And coming.

Before he knew it, he was making a full-time living doing motion graphics as a freelancer.

But this wasn't his plan.

His big goal was to get a few years of professional experience at a studio and then strike out on his own.

But with the apartment fire in the back of his mind, he thought, *Why wait?*

He stopped applying for studio jobs and decided to invest everything he had into his freelance business. "If things fall apart," he reasoned, "I can always go get a job if I need to."

"IT'S LIKE MY FAVORITE THING TO DO."

Things didn't fall apart.

But there were a lot of ups and downs, especially when it came to steady income.

To help with that, Austin decided to create his own digital product.

> *I didn't want to just trade time for money, because that's not scalable. I wanted to do something that was potentially scalable, to even the ups and downs of freelance.*

He knew people would be most interested in an online course for lettering animation, something he was doing a lot of and people were asking about. But there was one big problem.

Austin didn't think he was good enough, especially at teaching.

In fact, he always said he'd *never* be a teacher.

Austin tells me that he *also* always said he'd *never* own a Ford Taurus. Or work at a software company. Or sit behind a computer.

And yet—after college he drove a Ford Taurus every day to his job at a software company where he sat behind a computer.

That was a formative time in his life. It's where he fell in love with motion graphics. And it's where he learned to keep an open mind.

> ❝
> # He started an email list without much of a plan.

Turns out, I didn't hate the Ford Taurus, and I didn't hate working at a software company. The things that I feared and said I'd never do, I didn't hate and actually ended up getting a lot out of.

What if teaching would be the same?

He built his first online course.

He fell in *love* with teaching. "It's like my favorite thing to do," he tells me.

It seems like everything he declares he'll never do he ends up doing and loving. He then says, not so much to me as to the universe: "I would like to declare that I never want to be wealthy or terribly successful."

We laugh.

"FEAR WILL ALWAYS BE THERE."

Austin was glad he grew an email list for two years; he had 1,000 people who would potentially be interested in his first course, *The Lettering Animation Course.* All he had to do now was write the emails and hit send.

Easy.

Right?

But for Austin, that's when imposter syndrome interferes.

He freezes.

He doesn't want to hit send.

Then he remembers what Elizabeth Gilbert said about fear in the book *Big Magic,* paraphrasing:

Fear's always going to be with you. Invite it on the car ride. Say, come on, we're taking a trip. "Come on Fear you're allowed in the car, but you have to sit in the back. And under no circumstances can you give directions, touch the radio, say anything. You can come along for the ride, but you have to shut up."

However, sometimes the second you have even an idea for a new creative "trip," fear races to the driver's seat too. What happens when fear gets there first?

For Austin, it's all about recognizing the specific road signs that appear when fear drives his creative car.

> ## " The things that I feared and said I'd never do, I didn't hate and actually ended up getting a lot out of.

When fear starts creeping in, I almost never hear a voice that says "Stop." It always comes in the form of feeling nauseous and the tug of, "The dishes are dirty."

I can feel myself slowly getting pulled away from the thing I know is important, until it almost becomes like I've forgotten about it. I think stalling is fear's better tactic for me. Because I fall for it. It's recognizing that the distractions are what fear is making me do.

Once he realizes fear is driving—because he sees through the tricks—he calls fear out and kicks it to the backseat: "Okay, that was fear doing that," he'll say to himself. "No more. I'm going to stay focused—you get in the backseat and shut up."

It's something he's had to do over and over again.

He used to be scared of emailing 100 people. And as his list grew, so did the fear.

Embarrassment meant he'd beaten procrastination and perfectionism.

But eventually, he became thankful for the constant battle, always having to tell fear to get behind him.

> *Fear will always be there. It's not going to magically go away. But I think if I never feel imposter syndrome again, that means I'm not trying to push myself and grow.*

"IT WAS GOOD TO FEEL EMBARRASSED."

Austin also struggles with perfectionism.

He kept putting off launching his course.

He wanted things to be "perfect."

He, or rather fear, kept giving him a million boxes to check before he could move forward: he couldn't launch until his email list was bigger, he couldn't launch until he was more comfortable with teaching—until, until, until.

Fear again. He knew how to beat it this time.

He created a landing page.

It said: "In two months, I'm launching a lettering animation course. Sign up to get notified when it's available."

People started signing up.

Only problem was, two months later, the course *wasn't* ready.

Austin felt embarrassed.

Now he had to tell everyone it wasn't ready.

But before he could fall into a shame spiral and regret ever telling anyone his goals, he stopped himself and appreciated the moment, appreciated the embarrassment. He thought about what feeling embarrassed really meant.

Embarrassment meant he'd beaten procrastination and perfectionism.

Embarrassment was a sign he was still on the right track. "It was good to feel embarrassed because it also showed me that I wanted to actually do it."

His motivation grew, and not long after his original two-month deadline, he launched the course to his email list of about 1,300 people.

He sent the first email.

And waited.

And waited.

Thirty minutes went by.

Nothing.

Fear started to grab the wheel.

But then that first sale came through. And with it another, and another. Each one speaking *for* Austin this time, telling fear to get back with every email notification.

> *I'm glad I didn't listen to people who said "email is dead." Because I don't know where I'd be.*

As social media algorithms changed over the years, Austin watched his Twitter and Instagram growth slow, "but my email list still goes up and up and up. And I can own that."

A total of 3% of Austin's email list purchased his $400 course. He made $16,500.

> *It just blew my mind. I'd never made that much on any project. It gave me the confidence that this can work.*

He couldn't wait to launch it again.

He did.

BUSINESS BY THE NUMBERS

3,987 → EMAIL LIST SUBSCRIBERS

35% → AVERAGE OPEN RATE

5.5K → MONTHLY PAGE VIEWS

REVENUE BREAKDOWN

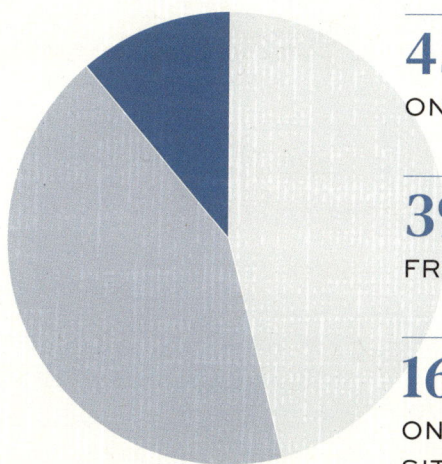

45%
ONLINE COURSE SALES

39%
FREELANCE CLIENTS

16%
ONLINE MEMBERSHIP SITE

But the second time, only 2% of his list bought the course.

He was crushed.

"I'M HERE TO HELP THE PEOPLE WHO WANT TO BE HELPED."

Fear rubbed its hands in delight and started whispering doubt into Austin's head, backseat driving:

Oh, I screwed up. What's going wrong? That's a bad trend. Things are only going to get worse now.

Sometimes, we cannot shut fear up alone. Sometimes, we need our friends.

We need stories.

Austin's friends told him stories of their own second launches, and helped him put the numbers into context.

If you have had a list for a long time (like I had), you're going to have a bigger percentage of people buy because no one's had an opportunity to buy anything from you. The wealth of potential buyers is building and building and building. The first time you launch, it releases the pressure and a lot of people buy. But the second time there's not quite as much of a buildup of people.

I realized that continuously building the list is very important. I can't just rest on the same list of people, right? Because not everybody's going to buy, not even eventually. I have to get new fresh people in there.

That was one of the big things that I learned after the first two launches—building a list needs to be a continual thing.

Then he tells me how much he actually made in his second launch: $18,000.

His numbers actually were going *up*. We laugh at how ridiculously easy it is for fear to blind us sometimes, to make us think the sky is falling when, really, we're doing *great*.

Like how *one* silly email reply can send us spiraling, confirming all our worst fears.

During one launch, Austin remembers getting an email about how many emails he was sending. It said:

Stop doing this. You're going to go out of business if you keep doing this.

But before he could let that take him down, he remembered the *dozens* of replies he was getting like this:

Thank you so much for sending all these emails; I've wanted to do this. And it took me reading all of these emails to make the decision to go for it.

When Austin writes launch emails now, he thinks:

I'm doing this for the people who need that push, who want to make a change in their life by learning a new skill. I'm not going to stop emailing a bunch; anybody's free to unsubscribe at any time. I'm here to help the people who want to be helped.

Sounds like a driver telling fear who's boss.

Even his parents are shocked at the transformation.

My mom and dad have both said, "I cannot believe you love going to conferences, love meeting people, love getting on video calls and teaching people in a live capacity. That is not you." I was the shy person who didn't like to talk to anybody as a kid. And just totally not confident in myself.

While selling his course definitely helped him grow his confidence—"Money is an indicator that something's working and helping people"—he credits the two-year "slow build" of growing his email list and writing to his audience weekly for the real confidence change. Every time he hit "send" was a tally for him and a zero for fear. And as the tally marks grew, so did his sense of what he could do.

To stay inspired, and keep fear buckled in the back seat, Austin consumes "a constant stream of inspiration."

> *I need inspiration so, so much. I watch YouTube videos, I read blog posts, I watch Instagram stories from people who inspire me. Without inspiration externally, I have a difficult time staying motivated.*

I notice a very full bookshelf behind him, color-coded, with titles like

Creativity, Inc., *The Hate U Give*, *Harry Potter*, *Big Magic*.

There is also inspirational art on every wall, including a lettering piece by Dan Lee, phrases drawn close together, an army of sorts to help Austin every day:

"Take a positive step today."

"Buy a sketchbook and a pen."

"Do not be critical."

"Just turn the page and start another."

"No one else in the universe would have drawn it quite like you."

Austin looks at this piece every time he feels like he's not good enough. It reminds him that every morning he wakes up is another chance. ∎

141

Where beautiful art comes from

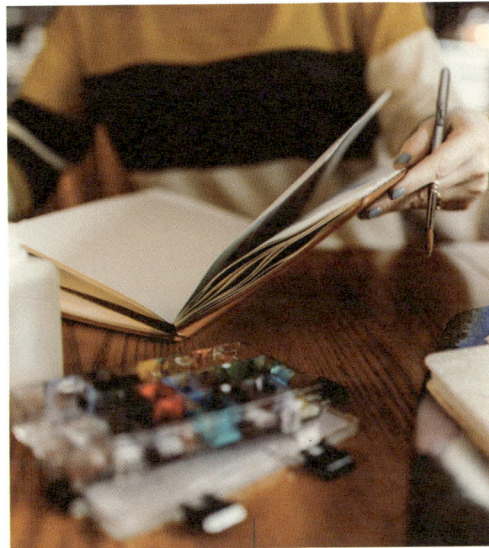

Watercolorist Angela Fehr never wanted to become one of those people who "used to" make art. Instead, she mixed her heart-guided approach, decades of mastering her craft, and a little "foolish" confidence to make a full-time living as an artist.

I was so afraid I would become one of those people who used to make art.

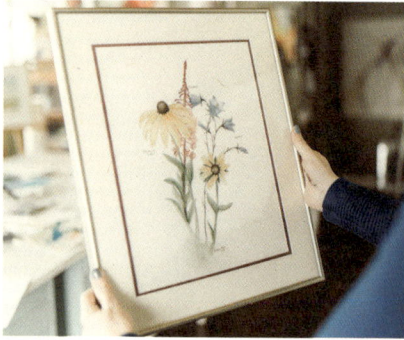

Angela's watercolor paints kept disappearing and she couldn't figure out why.

It wasn't until she saw, well, "pastel-colored cockroach turds on the floor" that she realized cockroaches were eating her paint—just another symptom of life in the jungle.

Angela grew up in Papua New Guinea with missionary parents from a small town in British Columbia, Canada. The jungle, even with the cockroaches, was where her creativity flourished.

She learned to improvise without a craft store nearby, and giant rolls of paper might as well have been pure gold.

I ask her about a giant roll of paper almost my height laying across her workspace—I recognize it from my own childhood garage (my mom used rolls like that for *everything*).

"I owe it all to those big rolls of paper," Angela tells me. They were the ultimate blank canvas. Endless blank space where anything could happen.

Angela is also grateful for all the women in her life whose unspoken motto was, "Here's some art supplies." Her grandma always let her use her sewing machine, and Angela was always encouraged to create.

When she turned 18 and moved back to Canada, Angela was so excited about the opportunity to take a real art class that she signed up for the very first one available at the community center in her small town in Northern British Columbia—it was a watercolor class.

She was the youngest in the class by about 50 years, but she loved the women there. Their encouragement meant everything to her, "because making art alone in the jungle, you have no idea if what you're making is good."

That community center watercolor class changed Angela forever, sparking a lifelong love affair with watercolor, coupled with a driving fear.

Angela met people who told her how they "used to do art *until*" they had kids or got busy or started working more hours.

> *I was terrified that that would be me. I was so afraid I would become one of those people who used to make art.*

At 18 years old, she was determined to find a way to never let that happen.

"I DIDN'T KNOW ANYBODY WHO WAS MAKING A FULL-TIME LIVING AS AN ARTIST."

Angela didn't think watercolor painting could be a career, though.

> *I had no plans of being an artist as a career because I didn't know anybody who was making a full-time living as an artist.*
>
> *Everybody I knew was either bankrolled by a spouse or doing it in retirement or as a hobby.*

Since she was both drawn to art and had a need to pay rent, she got a job as a graphic designer at the local print shop. Her boss was willing to train her and she began learning graphic design software. Graphic design was "the one job I thought an artist could have."

She started to "figure out the business side of art." And while she enjoyed the graphic design work, it wasn't enough:

> *I was being an artist, but I wasn't being the kind of artist I really wanted to be.*

So every night for two years after she got home from work, Angela painted in the evenings. Sitting on the couch with "everything just spread out around my lap," she intensely focused on growing her watercolor skills. She grew her business skills by day and her artistic skills by night.

Art was always more than a hobby for Angela, and even though she didn't think she could have a *career* in watercolor, she still approached it like a professional.

Part of that is simply the way she's wired:

> *I'm very business-minded. And I'm a little bit of a fool about it. I remember teaching myself to crochet and, after the very first thing I ever crocheted, I was like, "Wow, I should do this as a business and sell them."*

Angela's compulsion to turn anything she makes into a business isn't about money though.

It stems from an inherent drive to "always want to do more with stuff" and a compulsion to answer this question after she creates something new:

> *How can I get this out into the world?*

Naturally driven to share her art, it's no surprise that after creating her first full watercolor painting in 1998, a botanical floral, she thought: "This is good enough to put in the art gallery."

Angela jokes about her "foolish" confidence, but really it propelled her; belief, coupled with action, is *powerful*.

> *I think we're always waiting for permission, somebody to say you're good enough to grab that thing that you want so badly.*
>
> *And of course, when you're a teenager, it's your friends and family telling you you're good at art, but I didn't really believe them because they loved me. They'll like anything I make.*

How she felt about that botanical floral painting, Angela tells me, was different, pivotal. It was the first time she formed her *own* opinion of her work.

> *I needed that turning point where I decided.*

Angela knew, without a doubt, that she wanted to present her paintings professionally; following the feeling her work could be good enough to share, she looked up her town's local arts society. The week after she created her first full painting she applied for a membership and asked to show her painting in one of their art shows that happened twice a year.

They accepted, and once she built a collection from those two years of evening practice, they asked if she'd like to have her very own art show.

To Angela, showing her art in her small town was *everything*.

> *I'm a big fan of the way a small community can bring people together to create.*

She loved showing her art to others, and it further encouraged her to treat herself like a professional artist, and her art like a business, even though she knew it would be "very difficult to sell enough paintings to make a living" in a small farming community.

For Angela, even painting on the side was a huge win, a triumph over her biggest fear of being someone who *used to paint*.

Soon after that first art show, she got married and had three kids in three years.

She left her job to homeschool her kids full-time, and hoped her painting time wouldn't disappear completely.

"I MADE NAP TIME CREATIVITY TIME."

Angela remembers having three young kids as "a very busy time," and while she let the seasons change her artistic life as needed, she never let it stop her or make her feel less than.

147

> ## " I didn't have to sell anything. I could just share and build community.

I decided that I would feel good about my art if I could just get in 15 minutes a few times a week.

She did her own painting while her kids napped—"I made nap time creativity time"—and made sure she and her kids always had plenty of art supplies.

Her new target was to make three paintings a year, "and I usually met that target. So that felt good. It wasn't fading away."

Angela also stayed involved in her town's art community. She started reaching out to nearby towns that also had shows and entered local juried art competitions.

She didn't win any.

But that was really freeing for me, because I think if I'd gotten some success, I would have been really obsessed with, "What do other people want to see?"

It gave her relief to keep creating from her heart.

But there was also "a little secret part" of Angela's heart that thought, *I want to be a world-class artist.*

I knew some of the most famous watercolor artists in the world. I'd seen them in magazines and I dreamed of having that life, traveling the world and teaching and painting and having books published and all of those things, and yet I knew that was ridiculous. I was just a girl from a small town in the middle of nowhere.

Angela directed all her energy toward continuing to master the craft of watercolor. Even decades later, there was still so much to learn.

She noticed how many artists posted tutorials on YouTube, and in 2013, she grabbed a video camera for the first time and made a video of her own to share some of her watercolor learnings.

The camera angle was terrible and I didn't have a clue what I was doing. The kids were actually jumping on the trampoline outside the window, screaming.

But even with the imperfections, people connected with Angela's teaching. While she had, at this point, been studying watercolor for two decades, she still approached it as if it was the first day of her community center class: full of excitement, a hunger to learn, humility, and a deep love of art.

People were drawn to her approachability and the way she made watercolor feel so accessible. She

BUSINESS BY THE NUMBERS

15,781 → EMAIL LIST SUBSCRIBERS

70,000 → YOUTUBE SUBSCRIBERS

11,000 → ONLINE COURSE STUDENTS

REVENUE BREAKDOWN

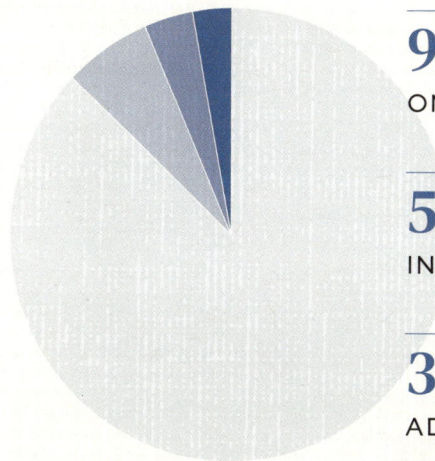

90%
ONLINE CLASSES

5%
IN-PERSON WORKSHOPS

3%
AD REVENUE

2%
ART SALES

brainstormed how else she might be able to help.

> *I wondered if there was a way to be more intentional about this and not just share random videos on YouTube. Maybe I could share in a more structured way and do a course or some kind of online class?*
>
> *At the time, I didn't know anybody who was painting or teaching online in any field. Online instruction was kind of just getting started.*

So she started searching the internet and found a site that would allow her to host a course and she thought, "What do I have to lose?"

"I SEND MY QUARTERLY EMAIL ONCE A YEAR."

Because Angela already built a small audience with her YouTube videos, people signed up for her course *Watercolour Mastery*; she was thrilled.

> *It was really, really powerful to see that I was now actually monetizing my time and going from that stay-at-home mom to someone who was contributing.*

Angela also had an email list back then—she started collecting email addresses in 2002.

It started slow.

She had intentions to send a quarterly email but would often joke that "I send my quarterly email once a year."

But then she'd sit down to write that annual email and panic.

> *I've got to pack all my year's news into one email. And then everybody who's on your email list forgets about you for the rest of the year.*

Once her first course started selling, she decided she would start emailing her list every week.

> *I think that really, really helped my business. It was so freeing because I didn't have to cram. I could give a little quick tip or like 'This is something to encourage you about watercolor today.' I didn't have to sell anything. I could just share and build community. And it felt so nice that I just committed. I have almost never missed a week.*

Angela's unwavering commitment stems from the joy she's found.

> *Writing my emails is one of the most fun things I do. It kind of brings me back to my days as a teenager in Papua New Guinea when I had to write letters because all my friends lived in Canada. That's the way I write to my audience now, naturally, just the way I would speak.*

> *If someone has taken the time to sign up for my mailing list, I know they know I'm a watercolor person, that I advocate this fearless, heart-guided approach to watercolor, and they're drawn to it; so I know I can speak directly, as though they know me, because they do.*

And she doesn't follow typical email jargon or formulas.

> *I really have a phobia of systems. There's a lot of stuff out there that says, "Here's what every email should include." But what has worked the best is just sharing who I am and thinking about the people on the other end, making it relevant to where they're at in their creative journey.*

She also writes for herself.

> *I come back to not just who my audience is, but continually question "Who am I? What do I need to hear?" And so actually, I'm thinking of my audience, but I'm also preaching to myself every day. Trying to stay heart-guided in my painting process means I have to give myself quite a few little pep talks and try to keep fear and doubt from crowding in.*

Because, despite her early confidence, fear still found a way in.

"I DIDN'T KNOW WHAT MY HEART ON THE PAPER WOULD LOOK LIKE."

Angela's course community is called "Fearless Artist," and her teaching is meant to help students reconcile with their fears so they can access the deepest places in their hearts, where beautiful art comes from. It's a scary place to go alone.

> *When I first started trying to paint from my heart, I wasn't sure people would understand. I didn't know what my heart on the paper would look like.*

Angela was terrified of being misunderstood, and every time she tried to paint from her deepest places, she heard a voice that said, *"Who do you think you are? You can't paint. Everything you do is derivative."*

But the internet, and how it "brings more artists into your home," helped Angela overcome those fears, which is why she's so dedicated to doing the same for others with her courses.

Angela's online teachers had a major impact on her artistic approach.

"These online teachers painted in a style that really connected with me," she explains. "They had this level of trust in their audience that said, 'We don't have to spell every detail out in our paintings. We trust that you'll get it.' And to me, that message was

so powerful and I wanted that in my art too."

Angela wanted to stop an old pattern; she used to reach a certain point with a painting and think, *"'Oh, I wish I could call this painting finished just the way it is, but no one would understand it.' And then I'd just keep working on it and paint the life right out of it."*

She made a shift, perhaps imperceptible from the outside, but game-changing on the inside:

> *I'm going to paint from my heart even if no one gets it.*

Once she made that decision, her business really took off.

> *It's funny, people really connect with your work much more when you're painting from the heart and not trying to impress them with your technical skill.*

"TRUST IN THE PROCESS."

For a long time, Angela's family was a one-income family. Her husband supported them with a construction job, often working brutal winters, while she raised and taught their three kids.

But two years ago, Angela started making a full-time living with her work; her husband no longer works winters.

I'm going to paint from my heart even if no one gets it.

We have a family life that's much more flexible because I'm able to bring in this income. And that's been really good for our family. Something that was always a dream is now a reality.

Since their family is now home together in the winters, they always watch the weather for signs of a good snow day.

Angela is grateful for the time together; she tells me about an email reply she got once from a woman who'd recently lost her husband and her biggest fan.

Now every time she tried to pick up a paintbrush, all she could think of was this man who cheered for her and supported her.

The woman thought painting would help her grief, but the grief paralyzed her. She was terrified of becoming someone who used to paint, and reached out to Angela for help.

Angela emailed her back:

Give it time. Art doesn't have to be your therapy. You have permission to not find it comforting right now.

Something that was always a dream is now a reality.

Angela is always encouraging her watercolor students to "trust in the process."

The tiny steps we make today feel small, and they don't feel like they're taking us anywhere. But you climb the mountain one step at a time; nobody tries to run up Everest.

So we trust that even when we can't see the destination, those little things we do, like those years I spent in graphic design and the letter-writing as a teenager, will take us where we want to go.

We can't manipulate the timeline, we can't choose when success comes to us, so there really does need to be that trust in the process, because worrying about it and trying to force it just doesn't make it happen any faster.

Angela and the widow emailed back and forth for a long time, becoming pen pals just like in her jungle days. And one day, when the time was right, when she was ready, the widow picked up a paintbrush again. ■

CHAPTER FOUR

Dreams come true

SOMETIMES DREAMS COME TRUE in a flash—a single moment that changes everything.

Sometimes they come true little by little, imperceptibly.

Sometimes it's a little bit of both.

These stories are about what happens when all the tiny invisible moments add up.

When a creator's body of work grows and grows, as does their skill, and somehow—miraculously, one day—everything changes.

At first glance, it can look like luck. Right place. Right time.

That's all true.

But for those willing to look even closer, following breadcrumbs, there are clues to something more.

And for each of these creators, the dream-come-true was never the end.

It was simply more fuel. A reminder of what they are capable of. And a fierce determination to pay it forward and show others what is possible when they take that brave step to create in the direction of their craziest dreams.

Building a legacy

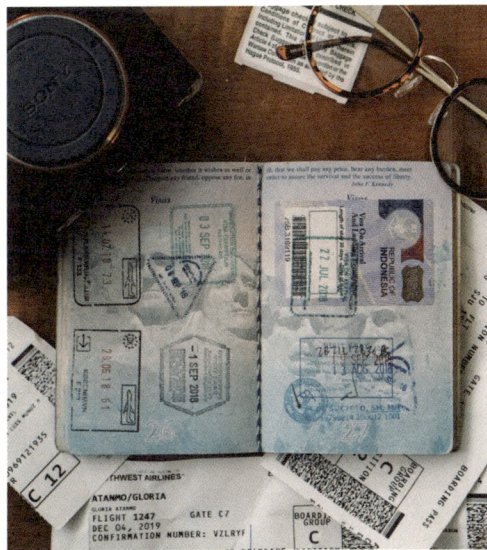

When you have no one to look to, you blaze
your own trails. Travel blogger Gloria Atanmo took
her future into her own hands and subsequently
paved the way for others to follow.

To Gloria Atanmo, "Travel was a rich kid's hobby." It wasn't something she ever envisioned herself doing.

In college, she traveled only locally for basketball and tennis as a double collegiate athlete at Baker University in Kansas. The athletics helped pay for school, where she started as a pre-med major as a way to make her mom happy. "She's the reason I'm here. All the privileges I'm afforded are because of her." But living someone else's dream was killing her slowly.

She quietly changed her major—even though it meant she'd have to stay in school for an extra two years. In her fifth year, her sports eligibility expired, and someone suggested she try studying abroad now that she had the time. Her initial reaction?

That's for "those" people. Natural-born travelers; rich people.

But Gloria—or Glo as she's also known— managed to silence that voice long enough to follow her curiosity and apply to a study abroad program; soon after, she was on a plane to spend an entire semester in the UK. The love was instant, and she couldn't wait to explore.

On her first solo trip to Scotland during a free weekend, she arrived too early to check in to her hostel, so instead, backpack and duffel in tow, she went on a hike she'd heard about—Arthur's Seat, an extinct volcano over 800 feet above sea level.

She got lost.

She'd unknowingly wandered off the path and into dangerous territory,

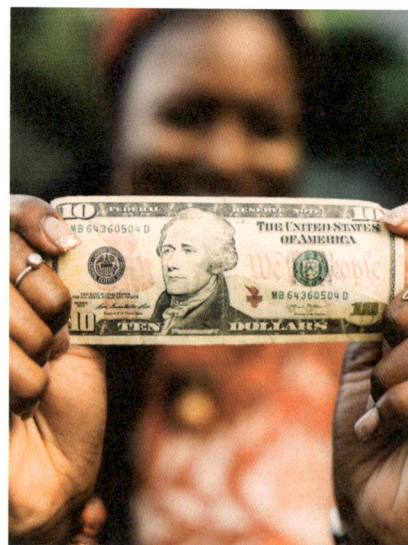

her bags weighing her down, pulling her in all directions, eventually trapping her in a ravine. She didn't know how she was going to get back.

Then she heard a voice from above.

"Throw your bag over! Throw your bag over!" A woman urgently shouted, "in her beautiful Scottish accent."

Glo threw her bags to the woman who guided her safely back down the mountain, out of harm's way.

The rescue was followed by a dinner invitation, which Glo accepted.

> *She made me dinner and sang traditional Scottish songs, and I remember thinking, "Am I in a movie?" But country after country, weekend after weekend, I kept having these serendipitous moments where strangers showed me how amazing and beautiful the world is.*

She found a deep sense of belonging doing the thing she never believed she deserved or was worthy of.

While the trip would end in a few months, Glo couldn't imagine this experience being relegated as a distant college memory. She resolved:

> *I don't know how, but I'm going to do this for as long as I can.*

"I GUESS I'M GOING TO BARCELONA."

Glo returned from the UK and finished her college degree. She was so scared to tell her mom she'd changed her major that she didn't tell her until 10 days before graduation. "She was *not* happy."

Glo ran away.

Kind of.

She'd made such a great impression on the university in the UK where she did her study abroad that she landed an internship there. She booked a one-way ticket back to Europe.

She also started her blog, *The Blog Abroad*. It was the first time she created a blog with a purpose beyond self-expression. She created her first · blog when she was 11 years old.

> *Oh my gosh, it was so embarrassing. It was on Xanga, and it was called "iMa_LiL_BLaQ_BaLLa_HoLLa."*

She wrote about school drama and boys. "It was very hard-hitting news," she laughs.

Blogging became a constant in Glo's life, as natural as reading or watching TV. While the platforms and the topics changed, she was always writing.

> *I had a pop culture blog, a music blog, a sports blog, a lifestyle blog, and then, eventually, a travel blog.*

"
I don't know how, but I'm going to do this for as long as I can.

She wanted to see if the travel blog could turn into a creative career. She saw other travelers and creators making a living doing work they loved, like *The Blonde Abroad* and *Nomadic Matt*, and their very existence inspired her: *"Okay, they're making it work, so at least I know that it's possible."*

And for Glo, that's all she needs to get started.

> *As long as I know there's a possibility it can happen, say no more; I will figure out the rest.*

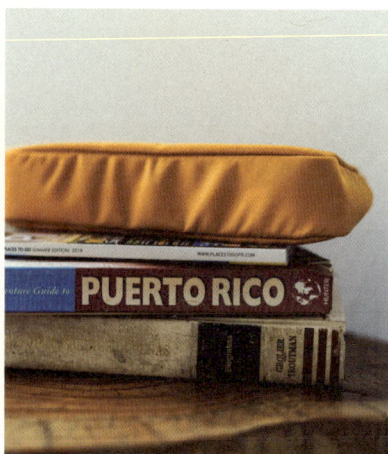

For six months, she became a kind of Clark Kent, working her UK internship by day, building her blog by night, often sleeping in her office, or sometimes not sleeping at all.

But when the college underwent serious budget cuts, despite how hard she worked and how much her boss wanted her to stay, her job disappeared.

With only one week left on her visa, she had to get out of the UK, and fast.

> *I looked at flights and found a $20 ticket to Barcelona and thought, "I guess I'm going to Barcelona." I've always been the kind of person who would rather make an imperfect decision quickly rather than stall and miss out on opportunities along the way.*

She landed in Spain with $100 in her bank account, found a hostel, and immediately started bartering to make ends meet.

For a while she survived on $10 a day.

> *Most people have their mom or their dad or someone to call in an emergency. But I just didn't have that privilege of being able to say, "Hey Mom, I've got $10 left, can I borrow a little something?" Nigerian parents raise you to be self-sufficient, so you fear and—quite frankly—wouldn't dare to ask or show your vulnerabilities to them.*

Glo is one of six kids. When she was 11 years old, her dad was deported to Nigeria.

> *He was given a 10-year ban before he'd be allowed to re-enter the country.*

For 10 years, Glo's mom, a nurse, raised Glo and her five siblings alone. Glo was 22 when the waiting period for her dad finally ended and he could apply to come back; but in that tenth year he tragically passed away in a diabetic coma.

So for Glo, while traveling, "there was never any backup."

"I'M GETTING THE MONEY, BUT THE TRAVEL IS NOW GONE."

Some days she didn't eat.

"

As long as I know
there's a possibility
it can happen, say
no more; I will figure
out the rest.

<blockquote>
It doesn't matter how much money you are making if your heart isn't happy…
</blockquote>

But she knew this phase wouldn't last forever. She was a hard worker. She was a creator. The starving-artist phase was something she both fully anticipated and was prepared to endure; her dream was worth it.

To make ends meet, she worked the reception desk at a hostel in exchange for a bed each night and did some social media management for a local restaurant. She also promoted food tours, did English tutoring, au paired for a couple of families—whatever she could. During one tutoring session, the father of a student found out she used to play basketball and encouraged her to try out for the Barcelona team.

Always looking for an opportunity to keep traveling, Glo borrowed some oversized athletic shoes from a friend and went to tryouts the next day. They signed her that night, and she became a salaried semi-pro basketball player in Barcelona.

She was grateful to be making a salary in a beautiful country, but staying in one place for too long—even a beautiful place—wore on her.

I wasn't able to travel. We were practicing three to four times a week, and on weekends we had games. So all of a sudden, I'm getting the money, but the travel is now gone.

It felt like her early college days happening all over again, her life taken over by sports—no time for anything else. The money wasn't enough, because money was never her priority.

It doesn't matter how much money you are making if your heart isn't happy with the circumstances.

After the season ended, she just knew, "I can't do this again. I need to be on the road." She booked a one-way ticket to Paris with one goal in mind.

I'm just going to keep traveling and see how long I can last. I need to get out there and create content, experience cultures, and continue building my brand.

"STOP ASKING ME HOW I AFFORD TO TRAVEL."

Without a full-time job, Glo went all in on creating content for her blog that might help her turn it into a business the way she'd seen others do. Through relentless content creation and learning, her blog started to make a little money via affiliate marketing. She was able to keep going.

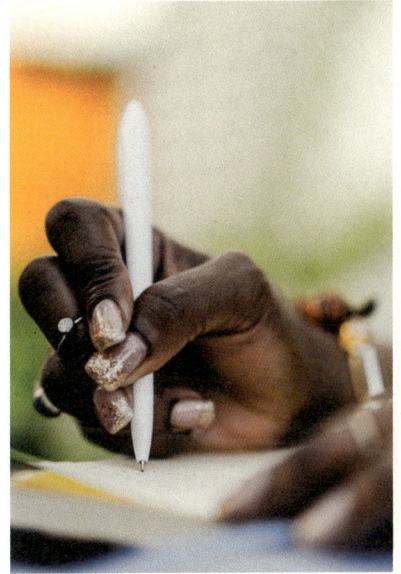

As a way to share her content even more broadly, she also started writing for other blogs and publications. In 2015, she became a contributor for *The Huffington Post* and wrote an article called, "Stop Asking Me How I Afford to Travel" that got half-a-million views in 24 hours.

> *It was this firestorm of people who either loved or hated it. I had never experienced anything like it. Followers going up by the hundreds per hour, and the hate comments felt like triple that, ha.*

The article was translated into eight languages and struck a chord with travelers tired of constantly explaining themselves. It also made travel seem possible for people who, like Glo, previously thought travel was only for "rich people."

The article captured the attention of a company in Germany; they emailed her: "Hey Glo, we found your blog, we love your writing, can we fly you to Germany? We'd love to work with you."

"DON'T TELL ANYONE I'M DOING THIS, BUT HERE'S WHAT YOU'RE ACTUALLY WORTH."

But the doubts soon followed.

Glo estimates she went through "two years of unnecessary struggle" trying to figure out what she was worth. One company would offer to pay one amount, then when she'd pitch that same amount to another company they'd be offended, chastising her, "Oh no, we would never pay that to *anybody*."

Glo researched, connecting with other creators to find out what they charged, and getting comfortable

"

Do it yourself;
own your story,
own your power,
and speak
your truth.

with her inherent worth and all that should be considered for valuation. For example, "Even if your follower count isn't that impressive, if you're a good writer, you can charge more."

Glo didn't know this right away though—it took time, and a very painful two years. Until one woman changed everything for her.

The woman worked for a travel brand and hired Glo to write four articles. When Glo sent over her pricing, she promptly emailed her back:

> Glo, don't tell anyone I'm doing this, but here's what you're actually worth.

She quadrupled Glo's going rate.

> I love her to death. She doesn't know how much that changed my life.

It empowered Glo to stop underselling herself; her dedication to that brand also quadrupled because of how fairly they valued her.

"I NEEDED TO PUT MY INCOME AND FINANCIAL STATUS BACK IN MY OWN HANDS."

In addition to brand partnerships, Glo also noticed the creators making a full-time living with their work seemed to operate a little differently than everyone else. They didn't compete with each other, but amplified each other's work; and instead of only relying on outside companies

or clients for their income, they took matters into their own hands.

Always attending conferences and keeping her finger on the pulse of her creative industry, Glo quickly noticed, "They were all creating their own products."

While the brand partnerships she had were going great, she was still struggling to make a consistent income. Her business model started to feel a lot like "waiting for brands to find me or desperately waiting on them to answer my pitches."

She decided to change course.

> I needed to put my income and financial status back in my own hands. I didn't want a brand to control how much I'm able to make in a year.

She started creating her own products, putting together her own group trips, and writing and self-publishing an ebook—"things that don't need permission from other people."

Her new business model? "Do it yourself; own your story, own your power, and speak your truth." Her income grew a little more every month.

"I REALIZED THERE WERE STILL SO MANY BLOGGERS OUT THERE WHO WERE STRUGGLING."

She also credits her income growth to her commitment to a "blue ocean"—focusing on a market that was virtually non-existent at the time.

I realized in 2017 that there weren't many Black female travel bloggers who were writing about some of the negative experiences—like being denied service at restaurants or being mistaken for a prostitute in certain countries.

I worried that if they experience this and think the whole world is like this they might never travel again. But if they see, "Oh no, this happened to Glo as well," then maybe they'd be inspired to keep going.

Glo wanted readers like her to know they weren't alone and that the beauty and adventure to behold far outweighed the horrors. She didn't want anything to stop them from traveling if it called to them the way it called to her.

With growing partnerships (like her dream-come-true sponsor, GoPro) and multiple products and offerings, she was able to scale her blog to six figures. But, just like that feeling of being in the same place for too long, soon it all started to feel too easy. She had spent *years* trying to learn how to make a living doing work she loved, and she'd finally figured it out.

Now what?

I realized there were still so many bloggers out there who were struggling.

Inspired by the woman at that company, she wanted to find a way to help them. She started transitioning her business from helping women travel to helping women see their worth and build the business of their dreams.

To do that, she focused even more on her own products and how to get them in front of the right people.

"LIKE A MIX OF A HEART ATTACK AND WINNING THE LOTTERY."

Glo avoided email in the early days.

I was a social media nut. But when I started offering premium products and higher tier items, like my retreats and my course, I realized people make business decisions through email.

So she finally decided to give email marketing a try for the launch of her Bali Blogger Bootcamp in 2017. She remembers the first time a sale came through: *"Oh my gosh—this works!"*

When I ask her how she thinks about email and social media now, her metaphor does not disappoint:

Social media is like a public swimming pool and email marketing is like the ocean.

They're both wet, but the ocean is just a different experience; if you're not getting wet in that way, then you're not even swimming.

You haven't reached the full potential of what's possible.

A pool is very safe, and it can also be confining—there are rules and hours you don't control. But email marketing feels limitless, like when you look out at the ocean.

Glo used social media and email together to launch her course, *Blog Like a Boss*. All her social media posts directed people to join her email list through a landing page that promised the top five tips for newbie bloggers. Once they signed up on the landing page, they received the automatic email sequence she set up, teaching some of her best strategies for free— establishing her expertise and giving her new subscribers a chance to get to know her and see if her course would be right for them.

It worked.

Glo made $50,000 in seven days, a culmination of years of hard work and almost two decades of blogging.

How did it feel?

Like a mix of a heart attack and winning the lottery.

"BECAUSE WHAT GOOD IS GETTING ALL THIS SUCCESS IF THERE'S NO ONE TO TURN AROUND AND HELP?"

Over 190 people have taken Glo's course so far, and she's gotten so

BUSINESS BY THE NUMBERS

11,319 → EMAIL LIST SUBSCRIBERS

32% → AVERAGE OPEN RATE

REVENUE BREAKDOWN

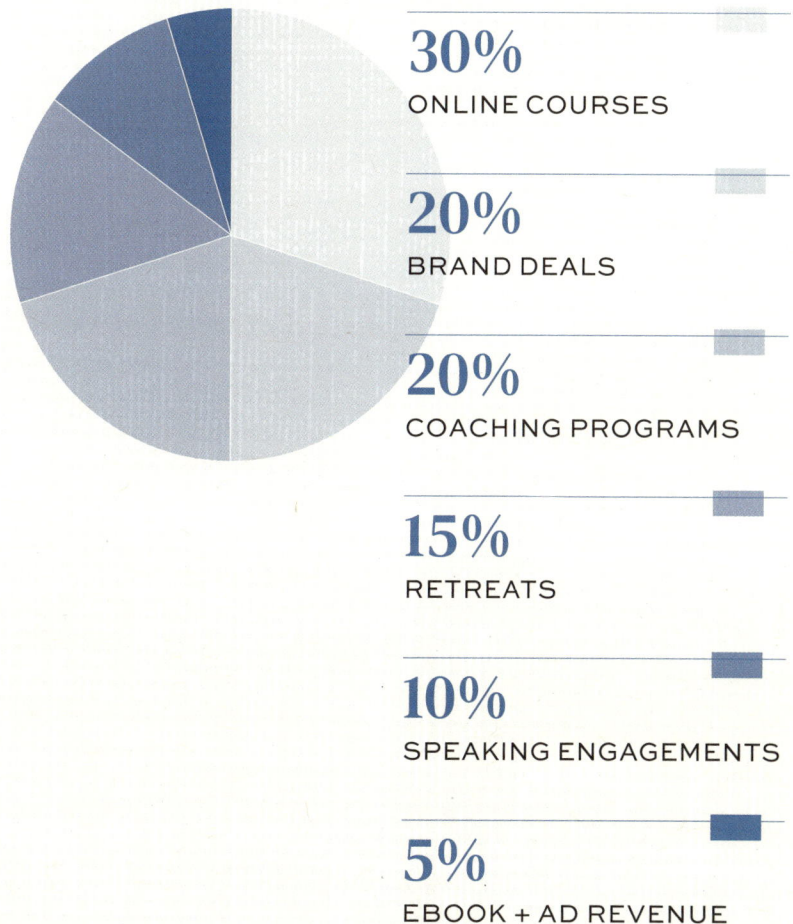

30%
ONLINE COURSES

20%
BRAND DEALS

20%
COACHING PROGRAMS

15%
RETREATS

10%
SPEAKING ENGAGEMENTS

5%
EBOOK + AD REVENUE

many thank-you messages from people whose lives have been changed the same way Glo's was when that former client went out of her way to show Glo what she was worth.

Glo designed her course with that exact hope. She wants to save her students from those two years she spent struggling with her worth, undercharging and undervaluing herself.

> *I show them the value of building products, how to control their destiny, how to value themselves, how to reverse pitch, and how to truly get themselves to the next level. Sometimes it just takes someone else saying, "Here's what's possible" for you to dream a little bit bigger.*

She's very transparent.

> *I show them everything, because it can be quite secretive in this industry. No one wants to share numbers, no one wants to share even contacts or strategies or ways that they were able to get what they got. And I'm just like, "Here's everything, here's how much I made from XYZ." Because what good is getting all this success if you don't turn around and help the next person?*

She's especially proud that her course has an 85% completion rate.

"THE MORE I GOT TO WORK, THE QUIETER THE VOICE BECAME."

But even with all the thank-you messages she receives, doubt still comes out to play sometimes.

> *Imposter syndrome is something I wake up next to every single morning, like "Good morning, Imposter Syndrome—would you like sugar in your coffee today?"*

Glo may offer it coffee but she doesn't offer it power. She works hard to keep her imposter syndrome from making any decisions. She's learned how to silence it when it's being too loud.

> *There's nothing more silencing than hard work—when the keyboard is banging I can't even hear imposter syndrome's chatter in the background. I realized over the years that the more I got to work, the quieter the voice became.*

And it's paying it forward that gives Glo her relentless drive to keep creating with her keyboard, even when things get hard, which of course, they always do.

> *Every time I'm ready to give up I'm like, "No, there's this vision, there's this legacy that I've got to fulfill. It's not done yet." I feel like as long as I'm on this earth breathing, I can't quit.* ∎

The side effects of dreaming big

For Grammy-nominated musician Dave Barnes,
the slow days in his creative journey were
the foundation to big, affirming, life-changing
moments that happened in an instant.

My first email address was shortnsweet22345@yahoo.com. Dave Barnes laughs when I tell him; he's familiar with email addresses like that because he's been collecting ones just like it for 20 years. His first email list came by way of clipboards in the back of music venues, hand-written handles of '90s identities.

In his two decades in the music business, Dave has written songs for artists like Tim McGraw, Carrie Underwood, and Reba McEntire. He's opened for Taylor Swift, Bonnie Raitt, John Mayer, Lady Antebellum, Hanson, and One Republic.

I'm sitting in Dave's studio, sur-rounded by stacks of old songwriting magazines, framed posters from performances at the famous Ryman Auditorium, awards from songs Dave wrote for Thomas Rhett, Billy Currington, and the one that was nominated for a Grammy with Blake Shelton.

I count six guitars and one banjo.

I scoot a little closer to the candle that's lit on the coffee table between us. Dave is sitting at his desk-slash-keyboard. I begin by asking him ques-tions about his long music career and how he's managed to do what so many dream of doing but so few accomplish: make a living in music.

"LONELY ONES / YOU AREN'T THE ONLY ONES."

It never occurred to Dave to *not* write songs when he picked up a guitar.

But he didn't think of himself as a songwriter.

He didn't know anyone who wrote songs for a living. He was just having fun, doing a thing he couldn't *not* do.

But one day spent wandering his college library changed everything.

He opened a magazine that caught his eye: *Performing Songwriter*. What he found in the pages was himself.

He read about people who made up lyrics while walking, who mulled over a chorus for *hours* until they got it right. It was a revelation; *he was like them*.

He was a songwriter. "Oh, this is a *thing*," he remembers thinking. That moment you realize the thing you love can be more than a hobby if

> ## That moment you realize the thing you love can be more than a hobby if you want it to be; that moment you realize you aren't alone in loving something.

you want it to be; that moment you realize you aren't alone in loving something.

The magazine revealed a community he desperately wanted to be a part of. He missed his next college class, lost in the magazine's pages, and from that moment on he was determined to direct the rest of his life to becoming a part of what he was reading.

"TEARS WE CRIED / BECOME A LULLABY / KEEP ON SINGING / JUST KEEP SINGING."

Dave wrote songs in all his free time—the only problem was he didn't think he had a good voice. So all his songs were written for his roommate.

But then he wrote a song his roommate refused to sing.

It was called "Sailor's Lullaby," and Dave's roommate said it was too special for him to take—he encouraged Dave to sing it.

Dave sang it and thought for the first time, "I sound pretty cool singing this." The song fit his voice well. The next thought came swiftly, almost a calling:

> *What would it be like to write more songs that felt like that?*

It was the first time he approached songwriting with the question that sparks every artist's journey: "What do I want to say?"

His next instinct was to share his voice, though he laughs when he remembers his early logic.

> *Hey, I've never sung in front of people. You know what I should do? Book a show!*

"WHO KNEW IT WOULD BE SO HARD / JUST TO BE MYSELF?"

It can be paralyzing when you feel like running in opposite directions at the exact same time. But what makes a creator is the willingness to live in that space.

Dave remembers the terror of the first time he held that space, his first time singing in front of other people.

> *It's like you've never walked before and literally people come to watch you learn to walk.*

His first show was at a church in Knoxville.

> *I was nervous out of my mind. My mom and dad came, and all these people I knew came, and all I could think was, "Why am I doing this? This is such a bad idea," but also at the same time feeling, "This is kind of fun."*

The show wasn't perfect. But it wasn't a total disaster either.

He didn't sense any fake praise or see pity in anyone's eyes. We laugh as he shares with relief that his parents didn't have the reaction he thought they might, something like: "We love you. You're the best. But let's not do that again."

It didn't matter that his voice wasn't perfect or that he "fell" a few times. People responded—they really liked the songs—and that was enough for Dave to keep going.

That night his drive ignited with a decision and a plan.

Decision: "I've *got* to figure out how to do this for a living."

Plan: "I'm just going to go until something just fricking catches on fire or falls off the rails."

"SO JUST KEEP / DREAMING IN, DREAMING IN / DREAMING IN ELECTRIC BLUE."

Dave moved to Nashville in 2001.

While we're surrounded by books in his studio (e.g. *Big Magic*, *The War of Art*, *The 500 Greatest Albums of All Time*), Dave spent most of his early days in Nashville reading liner notes.

He'd pull out the booklets in every CD to look for answers: *Who wrote the songs? Where did they record them? Who played in the band?* (You can learn a lot about yourself as an artist by noticing the "fine print" you're drawn to—fascinated by something most people pass over.)

Living in Nashville was like *Performing Songwriter* coming to life. Dave met other singer-songwriters for the first time—people with the same dream, the same drive.

> *I just loved that community.*

He also found himself in close proximity to artists making a living in music. The dream expanded: "I want to do what they're doing."

He loved the challenge, and despite the odds, he knew he wanted this with everything he had.

But first, he needed to find a way to pay the rent.

He made calls to collect on past-due invoices for a modeling agency, was an extra in a prison movie, and moved armoires for an antique store.

He played shows at night at small Nashville coffee shops.

Then Bebo Norman, a musician Dave played drums for in college, gave Dave's name to a producer, Ed Cash, who was looking for some assistant help in Nashville.

Dave did everything from babysitting Ed's kids to picking up lunch for everyone during a recording session. Seeing Dave's dedication and potential, Ed offered to help Dave record a five-song EP.

Soon after, a musician new to town, Matt Wertz, reached out to Dave and asked if he would open for him.

After only a year in Nashville, Dave was an opening act with an EP to sell. He remembers jokingly what it felt like to sell something like 100 CDs after a show, making $1,000 in one night in his early 20's: *"The world is mine!"*

"IT SEEMS TO ME THAT DREAMS I TEND TO DREAM / ALL HAPPEN IN SLOW MOTION."

While in retrospect it seems like things happened fast for Dave, he admits that, "At the time, it felt slow," a side effect of dreaming big.

But the slow times are when momentum builds. You just can't see it yet.

How did Dave get through all the waiting and doubt, aka, the lugging-armoires-and-getting-people-coffee phase?

Step one: Mitigate the likelihood that decisions will be made in financial panic.

He kept his overhead low.

> *My rent was $300, and I had a beat-up car that helped me survive the slow lane.*

Step two: Remind yourself that this pace is part of it.

Dave constantly reminded himself of the facts: "This stuff just takes time."

He booked shows. He tried to get better—especially at singing.

People came up to him after shows to tell him that they liked his music. "Okay, and *breathe*," he remembers feeling, the doubt melting away, at least for a day. It's hard for doubt to ignore the evidence. And he was about to be presented with life-changing evidence.

"'CAUSE SOMEBODY, 'CAUSE SOMEBODY / SOMEBODY'S GONNA LOVE YOU."

In 2005, Dave walked into a bookstore with a friend. There was a book signing that day, and a woman standing near the author table called out to them: "Hey, come check this book out! It'd be a great Mother's Day gift!"

As they walked closer, Dave whispered frantically to his friend: "Dude, that's Amy Grant. That's Amy *Grant*!"

The woman hyping her friend's new book was Amy Grant, a six-time Grammy-award-winning singer-songwriter who'd sold 30 million albums worldwide.

Most things in a creative journey *do* happen slowly—but they build the foundation for the life-changing moments that happen *fast*.

In an act of boldness, fueled by adrenaline, Dave ran to his car to grab his CD, his first album.

And 20 years later, he's still reminding himself. He stops halfway through this reminiscing and says:

> *I'm listening to what I'm saying right now like, "Hear it again, Dave!"*

He sings the last phrase with gospel-like melody.

I ask him when he started to make a full-time living as a singer-songwriter.

> *I'm still figuring that out today. Today's the day.*

We laugh. Because we know it's true.

Even when things felt slow, Dave always kept going. It felt a lot like waiting, but it wasn't passive. He wrote. He sang. He met people.

He approached Amy: "Hey, I know this is weird, but…"

He told her about a mutual connection they had in the industry and how highly other artists spoke of her. And then, the moment of bravery: "I'm a singer-songwriter too, here's my record." He handed her his CD. "It was weird," he remembers. But he did it anyway.

Amy's reaction?

Oh my gosh, Dave, this is great. Thank you for giving me this! I'll listen to it today.

"Okay," he remembers thinking.

Two days later, a friend walked up to him at church and said, "Hey, I was just at this Amy Grant show and she was talking about you on stage."

Dave responded, "I'm sorry, all of that just went 'wah wah,'" like the librarian in Charlie Brown. He asked his friend to repeat.

"From the stage," his friend explained, "Amy said, 'This is why I love Nashville. I meet these people, and this guy Dave Barnes—I've been obsessed with his record. I'm trying to find him. So if you know him, find me after the show.'"

Amy Grant was looking for Dave.

He called everyone he knew who might have a connection with Amy and finally got in touch with someone who agreed to connect them.

The next day, Dave's phone rang.

"Hello? Dave? It's Amy." Before he could speak, she stopped him.

You just need to listen for a second. I can't tell you how much I've listened to this record. I am obsessed with it. I called probably 20 other Barnes' trying to find you in the phone book.

In that moment, all the waiting stopped feeling like waiting and started to look a lot more like building. "It was a big affirmation," he remembers, like something outside of him was saying, "Keep going. Keep going."

Amy and her husband—multi-Grammy-award-winner and country music legend Vince Gill—sang on Dave's second album.

"YOU CAN'T GIVE UP, GIVE IN, I SWEAR YOU'LL SEE / EVERY HOPE WILL COME TO BE."

It was as if the people Dave read about in *Performing Songwriter* had stepped out of the pages to welcome him in.

And 20 years later, there's no mistaking he's part of it now. A few times in our interview he casually mentions people like his buddy Shay (of Dan + Shay) and his good friend Tyler (of Florida-Georgia Line), who also happens to be coming over right after

> ## Most things in a creative journey do happen slowly—but they build the foundation for the life-changing moments that happen fast.

I leave to be interviewed for Dave's soon-to-be released podcast.

He doesn't say their names like a name-dropper would, nor how a fan would, though it's clear he deeply admires their artistry.

This is his community, and these are his colleagues. His family. They are his dream-come-true.

He never dreamed, though, that one day he'd be honored by that community via the Grammys.

It all started when country superstar Blake Shelton heard Dave's song "God Gave Me You" on the radio. He loved it and recorded it on his next album. Then it got released as a single.

> *I felt like I was watching a movie of my own life because none of that was planned or even mildly expected. There was no sense of that when I started doing this; I had absolutely no concept that I was good enough to be at that level.*

Then one day his wife got an unexpected text from one of their friends in the music business that said:

> *What does it feel like to be married to a Grammy nominee?!*

It hadn't even occurred to them to watch the Grammy announcements; they were sitting at home watching *The Mentalist*. Dave's wife showed him the text.

He cried.

Then he made some calls to make sure it was really true.

It was.

Dave's whole family went out to LA for the Grammys. It was a magical night.

But it also created new doubt.

For the first time, Dave wondered if he was capable of more than even *he* believed. (On the Grammys red carpet when an interviewer asked, "Tell us what you're doing here today!" Dave answered, "I snuck in.")

After the Grammys, Dave couldn't help but wonder: "What do I do *now*?"

"SIGN UP FOR THE NEWSLETTER!"

The answer?

Keep writing songs for the fans who'd loved him all along.

When I ask Dave if email has been a part of his life as a musician, even I am surprised by how he perks up in his chair and answers: "Always, always, *always*."

Dave started collecting email addresses after his first shows. "I'd leave some shows with hundreds of emails." He sent a lot of emails too.

His wife Annie was a subscriber in those early days, before they were even dating, and he jokes that she was probably rolling her eyes at his emails like, "Oh, man. *This* guy."

But for him, it was a priority from day one. "I was all about collecting emails and keeping people up to date." Social media didn't exist, and email was the only way you could truly stay up to date with an artist.

And even though the internet has changed drastically in the last 20 years, Dave has never stopped: "I've been sending emails for 20-plus years."

He still writes all the copy in his emails too.

I built my career on communication and accessibility. That was how I communicated from day one and it was integral to me that people knew that I was there. It's still important to me that people

BY THE NUMBERS

17,000	→	EMAIL LIST SUBSCRIBERS
10	→	ALBUMS
3	→	EPS

REVENUE BREAKDOWN

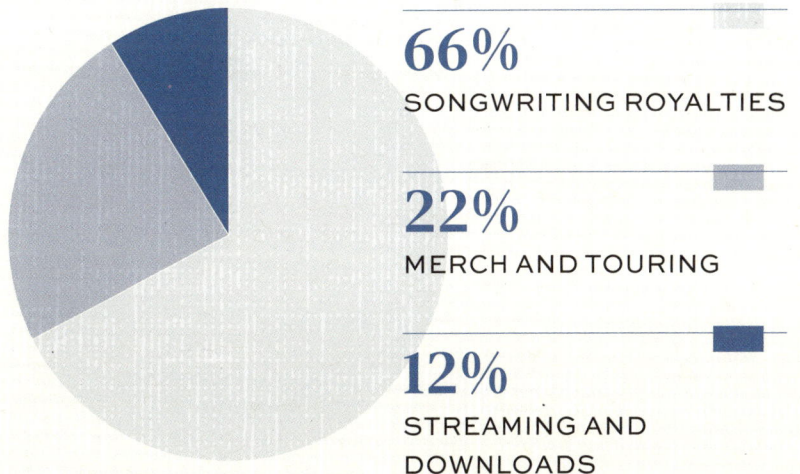

66%
SONGWRITING ROYALTIES

22%
MERCH AND TOURING

12%
STREAMING AND DOWNLOADS

feel like, "He's around and he'll respond to you."

"ALL OF THE GOODBYES / EVERY HEARTBREAK / THEY TURN TO MAGIC."

Before I leave this cozy music mecca to make sure my chair is free for Tyler, I ask Dave for any advice he has for creators who want to make a living doing something they love as much as he loves songwriting.

His answer:

> *Do your best to create things that really matter to people. I think that's how you build a long career.*

The people who really stick around, especially in the music industry, Dave observes, are the ones who have music that "really connects. That people feel is *necessary* in their life."

> *I think the best you can do is become a soundtrack in someone's life.*

But how do you know if what you're creating will matter to someone else?

You don't.

At least not right away.

All you can do when you're creating is ask yourself if it matters to you.

> *Do I feel like this matters? Does it move me in some way? Because when it does, it has a much better chance of moving everybody else. When I write songs, I'm the first listener, so if it doesn't matter to me, it's never going to matter to somebody else.*

Dave's fans play his songs at their weddings and as the background music to slideshows of their newborns. His songs become "theirs."

Dave knows that can't happen unless he keeps creating music that matters to him, letting it out into the world to give it the chance to matter to someone else.

And what keeps him grinding through that creative process after decades of ups and downs is the pure love of his craft.

> *When I write a song, I feel like I'm 10. You know? And sure, it's sometimes hard to get down to it, but every time I do, that magic is still there.* ■

No niche too small

Homesteader and author Deborah Niemann never dreamed her love of goats could turn into an online business, the ability to save goats all over the world, or help her find her security in her own self-reliance.

PHOTOGRAPHY BY → JESSICA WORLAND

The goats were dying. And Deborah had no idea why.

She was heartbroken every time she stepped out for a morning feeding on her homestead—32 acres "in the middle of nowhere" in Cornell, Illinois—only to find another lifeless goat. She'll never forget the pain of watching new baby goats fade away just hours after entering the world.

She called every vet she could find, crying, "You have to help me. I have to know why my goats are dying." Most told her sorry, they only saw dogs and cats.

She finally found a lab that agreed to help, but only if she performed a kind of goat autopsy. With the help of her youngest daughter, who was 12 at the time, Deborah grabbed a scalpel and began. When her daughter asked, "Do you know what you're doing?" Deborah replied, "Nope!"

Deborah successfully sent the lab what they needed, and before long she learned her goats had copper deficiency—a mystery and, it turns out, other goat owners were dealing with too. She did intensive research using the local university library and implemented what she learned to save her goats.

Deborah didn't know then that her dedication would evolve into an online business that would save goats all over the world.

"HOTELS DON'T ALLOW CHICKENS."

Deborah dreamed of having a homestead after she got pregnant with her first child. She wanted to eat really healthy, but in the early '90s it was hard to find health food stores in the Chicago suburbs where they lived, and what they could find was really expensive.

> *We started talking about moving to the country so we could grow our own food organically.*

She also loved the idea of her kids growing up in the country.

They talked about this dream for 13 years.

When her firstborn was 13-years-old, Deborah realized if she didn't move to the country now, her kids would never have the chance to actually "grow up" there. It was now or never.

They found 32 acres on a creek in Cornell, Illinois, 100 miles southwest of Chicago.

> *I walked around the property—32 acres is enormous when you're coming from a quarter acre lot in the suburbs—and I honestly felt like the queen of a small kingdom; I could go for a walk every day and never leave my property.*

Only Deborah was the kind of queen who worked the land, cared for the animals, and performed goat autopsies.

Her early homestead education very much resembled the emergency surgery with her daughter, a constant

> **Deborah didn't know then that her dedication would evolve into an online business that would save goats all over the world.**

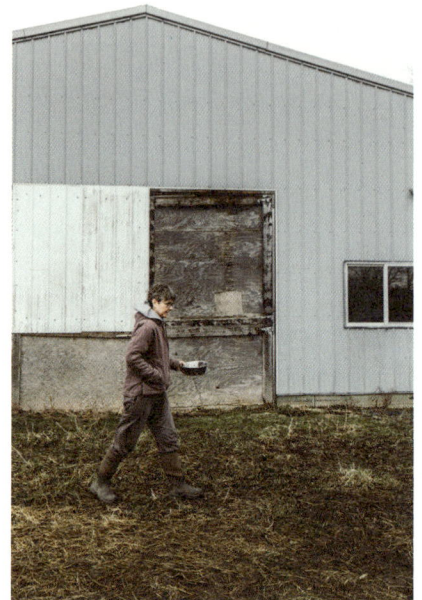

stream of: *Do you know what you're doing? Nope!*

But she never let that stop her. She read books on homesteading even before they moved to the country. A month before their move-in date, she bought 27 baby chicks and kept them in the basement of her suburban house until the move (she does not recommend this).

Those baby chicks were nestled in Deborah's car, parked outside her real estate agent's office, when she and her husband signed closing papers before moving into their new home. When they weren't sure about some of the stipulations in the paperwork, they thought about turning back—but then they looked outside and realized: "We have chickens in our car. We can't let this fall through

at this point. Hotels don't allow chickens."

"THAT'S A LOT OF PIGS."

They moved to the country that day to start their new homesteading adventure.

> *We were completely clueless. Our livestock experience to that point consisted of two cats and a poodle.*

When people heard about their big move to the country, they assumed Deborah and her husband had grown up on a farm. *Nope!* Well-meaning friends responded, concerned, "How are you going to know what to do?" Well, Deborah was going to figure it out. "This is what people have been doing since the beginning of time, right?"

Though of course, it was so much harder than she originally thought.

We made tons of mistakes.

But Deborah was not deterred. She made her rookie mistakes and learned from every single one, building up knowledge along the way and never forgetting what it felt like to start from scratch.

Most of the books she read were written by people who grew up on farms, so sometimes their advice was hard to follow. They would often forget to explain things that newbies would need to know in exact detail—things that were second-nature to them because of their upbringing.

So Deborah turned to the internet for answers. Was there anyone else out there like her trying this for the first time? It was 2002. She found and joined online groups: goat groups and chicken chats and farm forums, groups for soap making and cheese-making, and one just about turkeys. They helped.

She also noticed a lot of these newbie farmers were making money from their homesteading too. That sounded exciting. She kept learning and started experimenting with ways to make money. That Thanksgiving she sold 36 turkeys.

She got really excited when she learned one pig could sell for $700.

But then you start doing the math, and I realized that if I actually wanted to make a living at this, I would have to sell 100 pigs a year. That's a lot of pigs. Do I really want to raise 100 pigs a year? Not really.

What did Deborah *really* want to do?

"I THINK YOU MIGHT HAVE A BOOK IN YOU."

Her big dream since childhood was to be an author. She'd been writing all her life with this secret dream always in the back of her heart. "When my children were little, I wrote freelance for magazines, and I started writing for the web as soon as the web existed." She started her first blog in 2006.

She became known for her homesteading and would get phone calls like this: "Hey, my friend said that you're making your own soap. Can you teach me how to do that?"

Deborah's response? "Sure, come on over."

She had fun sharing her knowledge. People were always on her farm, learning how to make soap or cheese. She also started selling goats, and when buyers would come over to pick one up, she'd spend an hour with each person, teaching them everything about their new goat.

When it got to be too much to do all of that one-on-one, she started group farm classes—an old clunky cash register still sits on an antique table in her office, a relic from those days.

That's when I finally did the math and realized 'Oh my gosh, I'd make more money at McDonald's.'

Her classes were very popular, and she was asked to speak and teach outside her farm too; in 2010 she was asked to speak about bread at the very first Mother Earth News Fair in Seven Springs, Pennsylvania.

She was so nervous when she walked into the conference room for her talk. People were lining the walls—some were even sitting on the floor. It was packed.

A few minutes before it was time for her to step up to the podium, a woman approached her and said:

> *Hi, I know you're about to speak. I don't want to hijack you, but I just wanted to give you my card. I'm Heather Nicholson from New Society Publishers, and I want to make sure I get a chance to talk to you before the conference is over because I've read your blog and you're a great writer, and I think you might have a book in you.*

Deborah doesn't know how she got through her bread talk after that, but she did. She had been dreaming of writing a book for 20 years now. She met with the woman afterwards and was so excited that when the

publisher asked, "Do you think you can have it done in three months?" Deborah replied, "Sure!"

She couldn't even think about the logistics at the time because she was so thrilled.

> *But afterwards, I told my son and he said, "Wow, 80,000 words in three months, that's almost 1,000 words a day."*

That's when reality hit, but reality never scared Deborah.

She wrote for 12 hours a day, even during the holidays, and met the deadline; her dream came true.

> *It was beautiful and wonder-ful—right up until that part about getting rich and living happily ever after.*

Her childhood author-dream was akin to being a Judy Blume or Stephen King—making a full-time living writing books.

> *I never stopped to do the math until I was well into writing the second book and I had already signed my contract for the third book. That's when I finally did the*

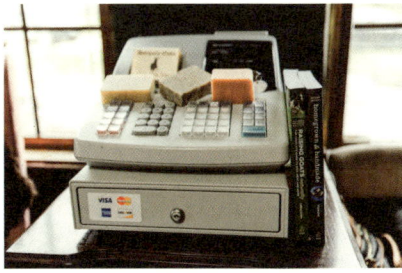

math and realized "Oh my gosh, I'd make more money at McDonald's."

And her books were doing *well*. They were selling. But, like the pigs, the math just didn't quite work. But unlike the pigs, Deborah loved writing.

I started thinking, "There's got to be another way to make money at this."

In 2013, she started teaching an online course on raising dairy goats sustainably (the topic of her third book) for the University of Massachusetts. But the math still wasn't working.

I was working so hard writing books, magazine articles, and teaching an online university course, and I would still make more money in fast food.

Up to this point, Deborah was a stay-at-home mom and her husband was the primary income provider. But as Deborah's kids—and her husband—got older, she felt a renewed motivation to make more income herself. "What if my husband died tomorrow?"

Deborah's husband is a cancer survivor, and she tells me that sadly both of his parents had cancer, and his mom died from it. She's so grateful her husband is healthy today; he even ran a half marathon in 2019, but it's hard for her to ignore the fear in the back of her mind that one day she could be a widow.

She wanted to know that she could support herself if she needed to. There had to be a better way.

"JUST NORMAL PEOPLE TEACHING PEOPLE."

That's when Deborah learned about online courses, what she saw as "just normal people teaching people—and not for college credit." The university courses she was teaching cost $1,000 at the time: "Your average person can't really afford that."

Online courses would open doors for her to teach even more people—and they wouldn't even have to come to the farm. She could finally retire that old cash register.

In 2015, she started creating her first online course. She laughs as she remembers the rookie mistakes she made there too.

At first, she thought she could simply repurpose her university class—but that style of teaching didn't translate to the online course world. Then, she thought: "Oh well, I'll just repurpose one of my on-farm classes." She asked her son to follow her around and film everything she did during her next class. She would just upload all those videos as her online course.

He followed her around all day with his iPhone, but the sound just didn't work. "An iPhone is fine if you're in your office, but it doesn't work if you're in a barn with animals making a bunch of noise."

She finally realized she'd have to start from scratch and make videos specific for this new online course.

"OH MY GOSH, THIS IS IT. THIS IS HOW YOU MAKE MONEY ONLINE."

It took her six months to make that first course. She called it *Goats 101*.

Before she launched, she read everything she could about launching an online course (she loved *Launch* by Jeff Walker). She was also inspired by Justin Rhodes who was in the homesteading online space at the time, selling things like DVDs on how to raise chickens. He made her think it could be possible for her to do this. She reached out to him asking for advice, and he recommended Nathan Barry's book *Authority*.

> *Before reading Nathan's book I had this really crazy idea that I didn't need to monetize my blog or collect email addresses. I just needed to get a book deal and then the "respectable" way to earn a living is to have people buy your book, and then you earn a living from that. But that doesn't work anymore.*

Deborah finally started collecting emails on her blog Thrifty Homesteader in 2016, and she was floored when 300 people signed up for her newsletter.

She's always looking for new ways to grow her email list and help her audience, and she loves using landing pages to test those ideas, like the free online course on goat copper deficiency she made that generated 800 new subscribers.

After spending time growing her list, reading up on the best launch strategies, and filming her course, Deborah was finally ready. She launched her course to her email list. Fifty people bought the course right away and she made $3,000—about the same amount as one year of book royalties.

I was just like, "Oh my gosh, this is it. This is how you make money online."

"I'M NOT WORRIED ANYMORE."

To date, over 3,000 people have taken her goat courses. But what keeps her going as "the goat lady" is the emails she gets that say, "You saved my goats' lives."

A month ago she got an email she'll never forget. It read:

I live in Myanmar, which used to be Burma, and I have an orphanage where I have 35 children who I take care of. I support the orphanage by raising goats. I can't afford to pay for your course, but my goats keep dying, and I was wondering if you can help me.

Just like the people who called her up in the early days asking her to teach them how to make soap, Deborah responded immediately, "Of course I'll help you!"

Her eyes water as she tells me about the impact this man had on the way she started to see her very niche business.

For some people, goats are just pets or a business. But for this man, every goat that dies is one

BUSINESS BY THE NUMBERS

5,700 → EMAIL LIST SUBSCRIBERS

30 GOATS   **12** PIGS

10 SHEEP   **80** CHICKENS

24 DUCKS   **1** LOOSE GOOSE!

REVENUE BREAKDOWN

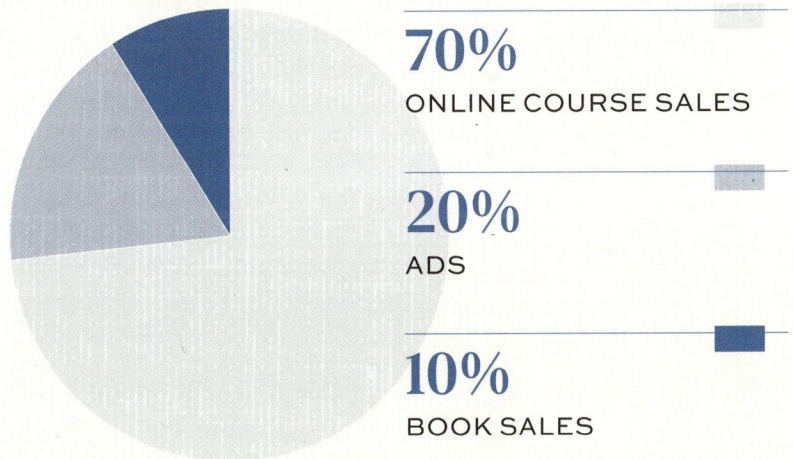

70%
ONLINE COURSE SALES

20%
ADS

10%
BOOK SALES

> ## As long as the world wants me to talk about goats, I'm going to talk about goats.

less goat he's going to be able to sell to be able to make money for his orphanage.

Deborah may not focus on goats forever, but "as long as the world wants me to talk about goats, I'm going to talk about goats."

The goats outside are starting to bleat, saying, according to Deborah, "Let us in!" The sun is casting a bright orange glow above the barn a few acres from her office window as it sets. It's almost time to let the goats into the barn for the night.

Deborah's 12-year old dog Porter is ready for bed too. He curls up beneath the nine bookshelves that almost fill her entire office as if it's a small-town library, a few of the books she's written nestled among the ones that helped her get her start.

And just above that old cash register is a framed picture of her and her husband on their wedding day; he's wearing a bright white tuxedo jacket, and she has permed, light-blonde curls puffing out from the top of her veil like a bouquet. I ask her how it feels now to know she can make income on her own.

I'm not worried anymore. I know I can do it, and it's really empowering. ∎

The long warm-up

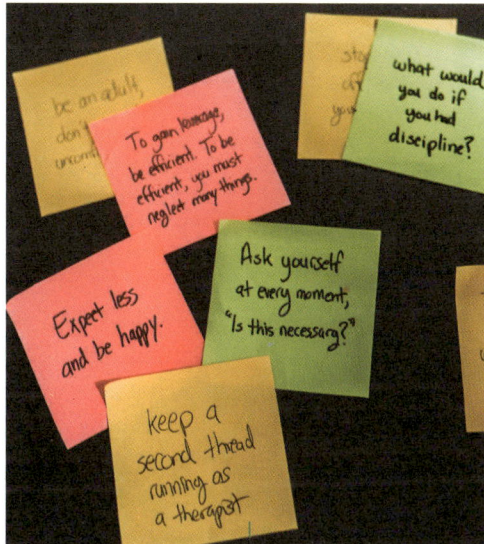

Parental encouragement can change a child's life.
With the you–can–do–anything confidence instilled
from his entrepreneur parents, *Indie Hackers* founder
Courtland Allen didn't let five years of failures and
burnout keep him from pursuing his dream.

When Courtland Allen was a kid, computers were his playground—literally. His mom owned a company that sold computer hardware during the 90's dot-com boom, and Courtland and his twin brother played there for hours:

> *If you put two bored kids in front of a bunch of computers, we're going to figure out how to install games and keep ourselves occupied. It wasn't that long before we knew more about how to use the computers than all the adults in the room.*

Environment is powerful, and all those adults kept telling Courtland, "You're so good at computers. You're going to be the next Bill Gates." Courtland had no idea who that was back then, but he used his computer skills to look it up: "Oh he's a programmer? I want to be a programmer, then."

By fifth grade, Courtland had a solid dream and a plan: "I want to go to a good school, and I want to learn how to code."

He admits he had no idea how to do either at the time, "but I was pretty sure that I would."

Courtland is contagiously optimistic. After you meet him, you find your biggest, craziest dream coming out from the dark. You didn't realize you'd been hiding it, but for the first time in a long time, you hold it in your hands and ask: *What if this is possible?*

Much of his faith in possibility (and luck) comes from his parents. His mom was a serial entrepreneur who always believed she could make her own way (and always did), and his dad was part of a furniture-building collective.

> *Both my parents were resolved to not follow the system or have a normal nine-to-five job. So, for me, it was always pretty normal to not go that route.*

If Courtland's family had a motto, it would be: "You can do anything." When Courtland played basketball, his dad told him he'd be the next Michael Jordan. When he started playing saxophone, his parents said, "You're going to be the next Kenny G."

But Courtland didn't want to be like Mike or Kenny. He wanted to be like Bill.

"THIS IS LIKE SOMETHING PEOPLE IN MOVIES GO TO."

But even with his big dream and optimistic outlook, Courtland was still shocked when he received an acceptance letter to MIT. After the elation wore off, he remembers thinking, "This is a mistake. I should not go here. This is like something people in movies go to."

But in some ways, his life would play out like a movie.

The call to adventure. Check.

Relentless failure? You bet.

Courtland's first five years of entrepreneurship were filled with rejection and failure. While at MIT, every idea he submitted to Y Combinator, a well-known incubator for early-stage startups, was rejected.

But he was encouraged by every rejection email; he never got a form rejection letter. Instead, he got custom feedback from the leaders of Y Combinator each time.

He remembers getting emails like, "Oh, I think this is cool. But you guys are all in school; you should finish school first. This is not promising enough for you to quit school." And, "Oh, I think this is kind of cool, but we already funded a company like this. It's a conflict of interest."

Courtland also got some rejection emails where they honestly told him it just wasn't a good idea. But getting any kind of feedback from people he admired was proof he was at least heading in the direction of his dreams. It was enough to keep him going.

> ## He looked at it all as 'a fun learning experience.'

Eventually, right after graduating from MIT, one of Courtland's business ideas won a business plan competition and he was able to live on that check for a year while he tried to get that business off the ground.

But the money ran out and the business didn't make any.

Courtland realized, "This company is dead." But again, he was not deterred. He didn't really process any of these business failings as personal failings. He looked at it all as "a fun learning experience."

With the end of that business, he moved to Silicon Valley to "be where the action's at," even though he had no job. His only plan was to apply to Y Combinator again and see what happened from there.

> *Best case scenario, I get in and that's great. Worst case scenario, I don't and then I just get a job and apply again.*

In Silicon Valley, Courtland quickly found a community, and soon, courtesy of the social news site Hacker News, he met someone to co-found a company with. They came up with an idea over coffee and applied to Y Combinator as partners.

They got in.

Courtland was about to be thrust into an environment where success was only counted in billions.

"EVENTUALLY, I JUST QUIT."

Courtland loved the energy and community of living in Silicon Valley (and still does), but it was also hard to ignore the prevailing doctrine of 2011: "Go big. Raise a ton of money, and don't care about charging customers. There's no real money in charging customers. First thing you need to do is get a billion users and then you can figure out your business model."

Courtland and his partner put all their energy into trying to get a billion users.

> *We tried, but it didn't really work. We got like 50,000 people, which is a lot of customers to get. But they were all paying zero dollars.*

And since they weren't meeting the big metrics investors were looking for, they didn't get any further funding once their incubator time ran out.

But then Courtland heard about this new company called Stripe—software that made it easy for startups to charge for software. It was so easy that Courtland decided they had nothing to lose.

Going against the business models he'd been taught up to that point, he thought, "Why don't we just slap this on our app and see what happens?"

They made $2,000 that weekend.

> ## " Sometimes the only way to keep going is to stop.

While that's nothing in Silicon Valley terms, to Courtland, it was everything. A revelation.

> *This is so cool. People are paying us money for this little widget we built! Who would've thought?*

But he was still so embedded in Silicon Valley culture that it didn't take long for the $2,000 to feel like nothing. Advisors said they needed to expand more. In hindsight, Courtland says he should have continued iterating on this thing that already had traction, but instead they shut it down to try to build something new —something that was built to make money from the start.

They worked on it for three years, but it didn't take off and Courtland got burnt out.

"Eventually, I just quit."

He was tired of struggling to make ends meet in such an expensive city. He needed a break, some time to recover from the "five-year gap of miserable startup failure" when nothing he tried worked.

Sometimes the only way to keep going is to stop.

"I CAME UP WITH A LOT OF GARBAGE IDEAS."

To make ends meet, Courtland became a contract web developer, coding and working from home and finally making consistent money. It was also the first time he'd ever worked less than 12 hours a day. He was able to finally come out of his hustle cave and spend time with friends, "enjoying the life I had not enjoyed the first couple years after college."

It refreshed him. But an entrepreneur at heart, it wasn't long before the drive to start something new returned. But first came the self-doubt.

I started feeling pretty bad about myself because I told myself I was going to be an entrepreneur. It wasn't my goal to just work for clients and make a cool salary. I was grateful for it, but it wasn't why I started.

He gathered his savings to use as a runway for his next business idea—even though he had no idea what it would be.

Using everything he learned in the last five years, Courtland made a checklist to help him find his next big idea.

It was a very personal checklist, based on all his "failings and mistakes" and what he knew he wanted this time around.

He wanted something he could launch quickly. It was the summer of 2016 and he only had enough saved to make it to March 2017.

He also didn't want to pick an idea that would require a lot of code:

I love to code, but if I work on something that requires a ton of code, I'll just code for eight months and not talk to anybody.

He knew he would need time to do other things like sales, and coding was a vortex he'd get lost in.

He wanted something he could easily explain to friends and family: "When no one gets what I'm doing, they can't be supportive because they don't even know what it is." That kind of support was important to him.

He also wanted to *really* like his customers.

I don't want to build something for customers I don't like because then I'm not going to like my job.

And he wanted to choose something that used his best skills—something to give him an edge over others who might be doing something similar.

Armed with his evaluation criteria, Courtland brainstormed like crazy. He evaluated each idea with his new rubric and spent three full days doing nothing but scouring for and scoring ideas.

Hacker News gave him a lot of inspiration, scrolling through endless forums to find stories of programmers who made their businesses work.

He brought every idea to his checklist. It wasn't great at first.

> *I came up with a lot of garbage ideas. Just a lot of really bad stuff that I'm so glad I didn't work on. But I'm glad I stuck through it because the ideas got better and better. By day three, most of my ideas were pretty good.*

> *We tend to think of ourselves as either good at something or bad at something, like "I'm good at ideas or I'm bad at ideas." But it turns out that you just need a warmup. If you do anything all day every day, eventually you'll get good at it.*

Of all the ideas Courtland considered, there was exactly one that checked every single box on his list.

"THE PROBLEM THEY HAVE IS THE SAME PROBLEM I HAVE."

During his research and ideation phase, Courtland had 20 tabs open at any given time; he spent days scrolling and scrolling through forums, reading thousands of comments looking for stories of programmers who'd successfully started a company.

He noticed many of the creators on these forums were looking for answers to the same questions he

" What if I curated stories that answered the exact questions people like me are having?

had, like, *What is your one-person SaaS business? How are you making money online as a developer?*

> *The problem they have is the same problem I have. They know they want to build a business, but they don't have any ideas. They don't know how to get started. They don't know how to generate revenue.*

Courtland noticed that people upvoted the stories people shared more than anything else—they found the real examples inspiring and instructive. But it took a lot of work (and time and scrolling) to find the good ones. Courtland wondered, *What if I curated stories that answered the exact questions people like me are having?*

The idea for *Indie Hackers* was born, and once Courtland saw it checked every single box, he got to work.

But the clock was ticking. He only had eight months until his savings ran out.

"

The hardest part of doing something new is not building it, but getting anyone to care.

"I KNEW I NEEDED TO START WITH MY AUDIENCE IN MIND."

To start, Courtland researched again, but this time, instead of reading forums for his own inspiration, he was out to deliberately understand *which* stories rose to the top and why.

He found patterns.

It almost felt like cheating, he recalls; the best research always feels that way. You can't believe all this gold is just sitting *right there*, for anyone to take.

You wonder how much you've been missing and wonder if anyone understands the beauty of what you've just found. But that's where all the creative energy comes from—you can't wait to employ your craft to connect and help others see what you see and feel what you're feeling.

Based on his observations, Courtland made a list of five things he wanted every story to have; things like telling the story in chronological order and sharing numbers transparently. All the effort he was putting in this time around made him realize what might have gone wrong in the past.

He doesn't think he spent enough time on research in his previous business ideas.

The hardest part of doing something new is not building it, but getting anyone to care. A lot of people build stuff—there are

billions of websites, but how many do you go to every day? Like five?

He recalls the painful past when he'd take six months to make something only to have no one care about it in the end.

So this time, I knew I needed to start with my audience in mind, to know who they are, what they care about, what they want, where they hang out, and what kind of messages resonate with them, and then work backwards from that—because that's the hard part. Once I got that figured out, then creating was pretty easy.

Courtland used his audience's top needs to craft his interview questions and emailed 140 entrepreneurs with an interview request.

"IT'S NOT LIKE YOU HAVE TO BE A GENIUS."

There was no copy-and-paste-then-change-the-name going on here. Courtland researched every creator he emailed and started each email with what he genuinely appreciated about them.

I sent 140 cold emails just to get my first 10 interviews on the site. That means 130 people didn't give me interviews.

Instead of thinking about the 130, though, he focused on the 10.

"But being an optimist doesn't mean you're immune to fear—you just choose hope when it does hit. But it still hits—hard.

He knows that without all those personalized emails he probably wouldn't have even gotten those 10. He reached out cold, asking people who didn't know him to be featured on something untested, unknown—something that didn't even exist yet.

He also used this email strategy when seeking advertisers.

> *Every sales email I sent was custom.*

And he worked to find the name of the person at each company most likely responsible for ad buys.

> *It's not like you have to be a genius—it's just how much time are you willing to research?*

There were some potential advertisers he didn't email, though, like Stripe; he considered them a dream company and he didn't want to email them until his site had really taken off and had the best possible chance of making a great first impression.

He sent about five custom emails per day while he built the site from scratch (yes—coding—he couldn't resist). But since he followed his list and chose something simple, a blog, he was able to code it in about three weeks, right on target. Now all he had to do was launch.

But being an optimist doesn't mean you're immune to fear—you just choose hope when it does hit. But it still hits—hard.

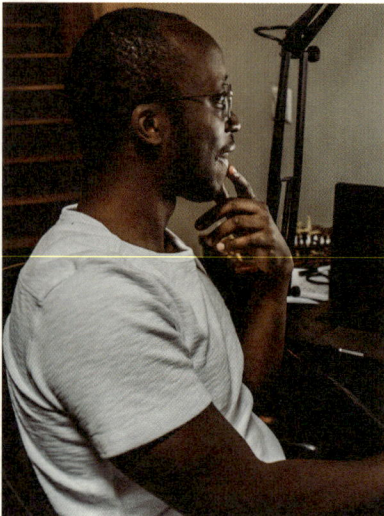

"EVERY DAY THE TRAFFIC WAS LOWER."

Courtland launched his site on *Hacker News* and that's when the fear hit: *What if no one reads this? What if no one cares? What if this stays at the bottom of* Hacker News *forever?*

It started at the bottom, and nothing happened.

But an hour later, it seemed all his research and all he implemented from the last five years of trial and error paid off—his site rose to the top of *Hacker News* with 100,000 pageviews in the first few days.

He doesn't remember sleeping much during that time—awake and high from the energy of his idea actually working.

But then, "this happened": Courtland shows me a graph that looks like it could also easily be the "Popularity of N'Sync's Christmas album from December to February."

People were loving the site—he was getting a ton of compliments—but once they'd read all the stories, there was no reason to return.

> *Every day the traffic was lower than it was the day before.*

Courtland started to get worried. His business model was advertising. He needed consistent traffic, and he knew those big spikes weren't enough to build a sustainable business.

That's where his email list came in.

"WITHIN A WEEK, I NO LONGER HAD TO COLD EMAIL PEOPLE."

At the end of each interview on his site, Courtland included a form asking people to join his email list to receive more interviews; with the attention his site got when he first launched, he had 1,000 email subscribers after his first week.

He also cleverly had a "Forum" link on his top menu—when people clicked on it they were taken to an email signup form that asked them to sign up to be the first to know when the forum was ready. Courtland hadn't even begun coding it yet, but he started collecting the emails of those interested right away.

BUSINESS BY THE NUMBERS

71,000	→	EMAIL LIST SUBSCRIBERS
45%	→	AVERAGE OPEN RATE
1.1M	→	MONTHLY PAGE VIEWS

REVENUE BREAKDOWN

stripe

100%
STRIPE

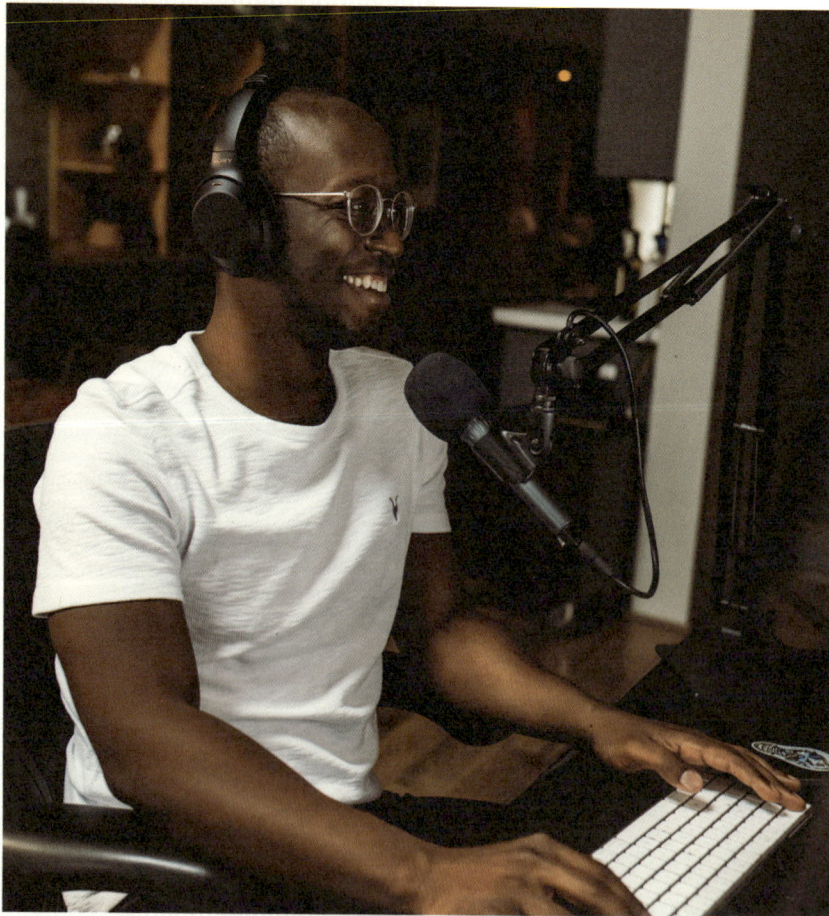

He emailed his list every Thursday. His emails were personal. He worked in public.

He took his list along for the startup ride. Each week he'd share the highs and the lows, new features based on their feedback, and new interviews.

Traffic rose steadily. The emails gave people a reason to come back.

It also changed the way he found people to interview; many of the people on his list were entrepreneurs already and replied to his emails asking to be interviewed.

> *Within a week, I no longer had to cold email people.*

He also found camaraderie and comfort from his list.

> *I would have probably just gone crazy by myself if I didn't have this email list that I was talking to. It felt like people were sort of working with me.*

Their replies became another rich source of research, helping him iterate along the way.

> *Even though it was just me alone in my apartment, I had all these people who were super connected and wanted to help.*

They felt like they were also a part of his story. Because they were.

In one email, Courtland wrote how scared he was about his advertising business model. He immediately got a reply from a guy on his email list asking where he could send Courtland a check for $800 to become his first advertiser simply "because he wanted to help."

"ACQUIRE *INDIE HACKERS*."

Despite traffic going well, if Courtland didn't get more advertisers, he was going to run out of money in March and have to shut down.

He focused all his time in December cold-emailing using his custom method. Money started trickling in. Slowly. He made $1,200 in December.

By February he made $4,000.

In March, he got invited to a wedding in Mexico. He decided he should take a break from work, trying to avoid that burnout that hit him years ago. But he couldn't resist checking his email at least one more time before he got off the plane.

He was shocked to see the name of Stripe's founder—Patrick Collison—in his inbox. The subject line? "Acquire *Indie Hackers*."

Courtland still hadn't emailed anyone from Stripe yet, waiting until he was "ready."

Turns out, Patrick thought he was more than ready. They believed in what Courtland was doing.

Patrick didn't want to change anything about *Indie Hackers* or take over or make Courtland a traditional employee. Stripe wanted to support *Indie Hackers* in the biggest way possible, allowing Courtland to take off his sales and advertising hat and instead focus all his time and energy on creating content that inspires more people to start businesses.

Courtland immediately forwarded Patrick's email to his girlfriend, mom, and brother.

"I WAS BLOWN AWAY."

After meeting Patrick and understanding what this could mean for *Indie Hackers*—and his life—he knew it was the best way to keep it going and have the time to invest in his biggest dreams for the site, like creating a community and starting a podcast. (Before I leave, Courtland gifts me with an *Indie Hackers* T-shirt and stickers that feature a beautiful custom-designed illustration of an astronaut holding a laptop to represent the *Indie Hackers* brand, physical proof of the kinds of community-building projects he was given the time to create.)

For that MIT kid from Georgia who moved to Silicon Valley with no money, no job, and lots of optimism, it was a dream come true.

"MY RULE NUMBER ONE: GIVE SUPER OPTIMISTIC, YOU-CAN-DO-ANYTHING ENCOURAGEMENT."

Though Courtland lives within walking distance of Stripe's headquarters, he calls a ride-share for us so we can make it there before lunch service ends. He still mostly works from home, but comes to Stripe once in a while to have lunch and meet with people. We arrive just in time, and the woman working the buffet of enchiladas lights up when she sees him: "Hey! We haven't seen you in a while!" They banter back and forth and laugh a lot.

After we eat he gives me a tour of the expansive, bright office space, and as we stroll through the library, just past a common area that looks very much like a lush greenhouse, I ask him what his dad, who believed he could be the best at whatever he did, thinks of all this.

That's when Courtland tells me his dad got sick just before he applied to MIT. The doctors didn't know what was wrong for the longest time. He was in and out of the hospital, spending four horrific months in the ICU. But Courtland tells me he was optimistic even then—he fully believed his dad was going to get better, every single day.

Until the day he died.

Courtland says losing his dad was like the dark mirror of the feeling of getting that Stripe email—a thing you absolutely didn't expect to happen that changes your whole life, forever.

We walk out Stripe's doors into the crisp San Francisco air and try to guess what Courtland's dad would think of where Courtland is today (Courtland's twin brother Channing also works on *Indie Hackers*). I smile as I think about how very, very proud he'd be—but also probably not surprised.

"If I'm ever a parent," Courtland muses, "that's my rule number one: give super optimistic, you-can-do-anything encouragement. I wouldn't have tried as hard if I didn't get that encouragement. I can directly trace it back to the people who believed in me. Because they believed in me, I believed in myself and did things that I would not have tried otherwise." ■

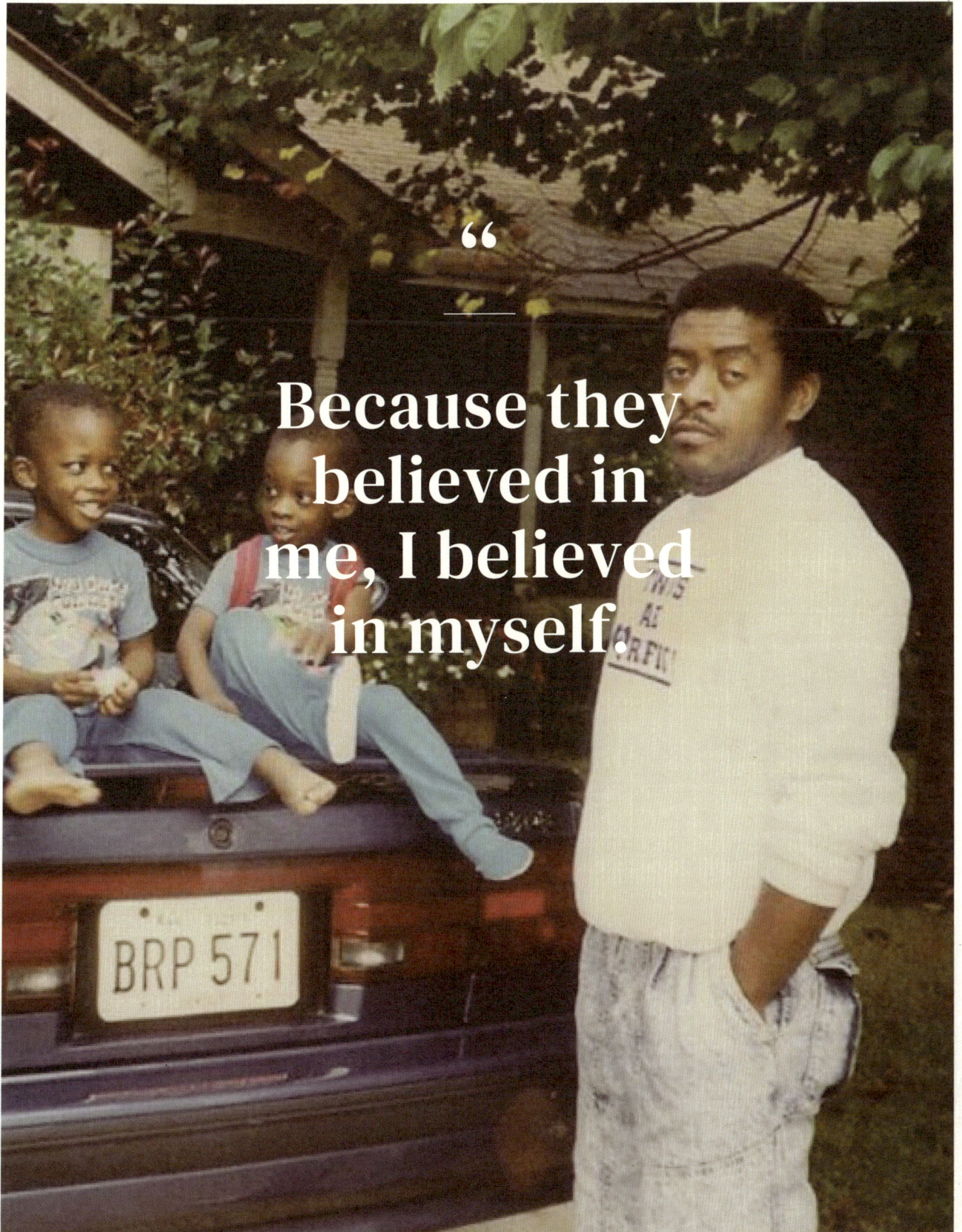

> "
> Because they
> believed in
> me, I believed
> in myself.

by Nathan Barry,
CEO of ConvertKit

The first few years of my life were spent growing up in a construction zone.

Just after I was born, my dad started to build our family home in the mountains outside Boise, Idaho. He recruited friends and family to help whenever possible, but he did the bulk of the work himself.

My parents, my three older siblings, and I moved into the house just after the sheeting went up on the walls—even before it had running water.

While it made for an unconventional childhood, I wouldn't ask for anything different. I loved living in that construction zone. I would sneak off with a hammer to pound nails into the floor in the most inconvenient places. Or toddle around with a tape measure, holding it up to random walls saying "feet and half!"

Thanks to my dad, being a creator is in my blood.

Looking back, building an entire house yourself without professional experience is pretty ambitious. Although, that's hindsight talking; what seems ambitious in the past is just plain scary in the present.

Whether you're staring down an empty homesite or a blank page, it feels daunting before you start. That feeling doesn't go away.

There isn't a single step in the creator's journey that's easy or effortless.

So why do we do it?

We do it to earn a living. To provide food and shelter for our families. But most importantly, we do it because we are creators. It's who we are.

The only question is this: Are we expressing our full creative potential, or are we still sitting on the sidelines waiting to start?

James Clear, the bestselling author of *Atomic Habits* (and also a close friend), says the number one habit that distinguishes the most successful creators from everyone else is that they start before they feel ready. Rather than waiting for the best idea, the right motivation, or the perfect conditions, the most successful creators just start.

I hope you see yourself in these 15 stories of successful creators who faced down their fears and took the bold step to start. I hope you start before you feel ready and become the creator you were meant to be.

Last year I set out to follow in my dad's footsteps and build my own house.

I started smaller and built a tiny house to use as my home office on our farm. I knew I could sketch ideas and refine designs forever, but it didn't feel real until I put up the first wall. The project took longer and was far more challenging than I expected, but it was also far more rewarding.

As I write this in the office I built myself, I'm so thankful for the example my dad set—he showed me what it means to take the leap, put up that first wall, and be a creator.

I hope the stories in this book set a similar example for you.

The future belongs to creators.

The future belongs to you.

It's time to start.

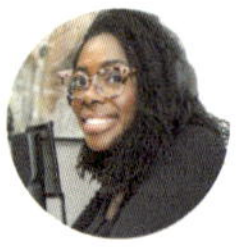

Jenell Stewart
Course creator
jenellbstewart.com

@jenellbstewart
@jenellbstewart

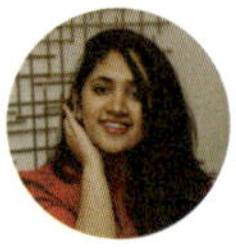

Chaitra Radhakrishna
Web designer + product
Photographer
itspinkpot.com

@pinkpot.studio
@pinkpotxo

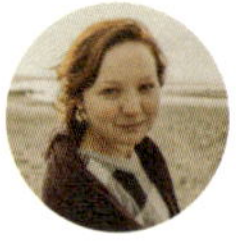

Jessica Bird
Writer
theserendipitylifestyle.com

@serendipitybird
@theserendipitycoach

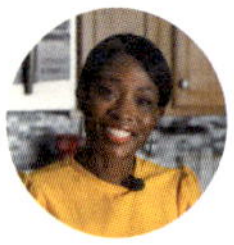

Tanya Harris
Food blogger
myforkinglife.com

@myforkinglife
@myforkinglife

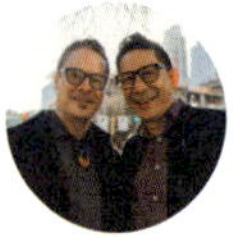

**Azul Terronez and
Steve Vannoy**
Author coaches + podcasters
authorswholead.com

@azulterronez
@steve.vannoy
@azulterronez
@stevevannoy

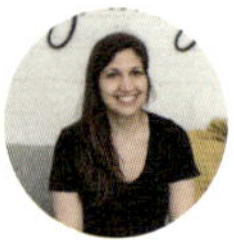

Teela Cunningham
Designer + hand letterer
every-tuesday.com

@everytuesday
youtube.com/everytues

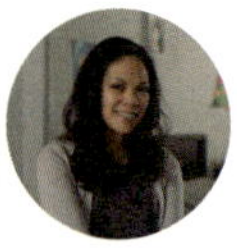

Nina Garcia
Parenting blogger
sleepingshouldbeeasy.com

@ssbeblog
@sleepingshouldbeeasy

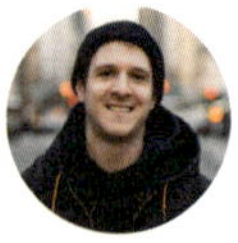

Eric Friedensohn
Muralist
efdotstudio.com

@efdot
@efdotstudio

Kimberly Brooks

Fine artist

kimberlybrooks.com

⊙ @kimberlybrooksartist

🐦 @1kimberlybrooks

Page 118

Austin Saylor

Motion designer

fullharbor.com

⊙ @fullharbor

🐦 @itsaustinsaylor

Page 130

Angela Fehr

Watercolorist

angelafehr.com

⊙ @angelfehr

🅕 @angelafehrarts

Page 144

Gloria Atanmo

Travel blogger

theblogabroad.com

⊙ @glographics

🐦 @gl0

Page 160

Dave Barnes

Musician

davebarnes.com

⊙ @davebarnesmusic

🐦 @davebarnesmusic

Page 174

Deborah Niemann

Homesteader + author

thriftyhomesteader.com

⊙ @thriftyhomesteader

🅕 @thriftyhomesteader

Page 186

Courtland Allen

Founder of *Indie Hackers*

indiehackers.com

⊙ @courtlandallen
@indie_hackers

🐦 @csallen
@indiehackers

Page 198

Rachel Renee
rachelreneephoto.com
@rachelreneephotographie
Page 34

Joel Stewart
jaynicephotos@gmail.com
@jay.nice.photos
Page 10

Greenhouse Photo + Co
ghphotoco.com
@greenhousephotoco
Page 22

Kaleen Enke
kaleenenke.com
@kaleenenkephoto
Page 78

Isadora Kosofsky
isadorakosofsky.com
@isadorakosofsky
Page 90, 118

Keith Pitts
keithmelissa.com
@keithmpitts
@keithandmelissa
Page 130

Karleigh Nickel
karleighnickelphotography.com
@karleighnickelphotography
Page 144

Jerome Stockton Fleming II
jeromefleming.com
@romeostockton
Page 48

Henry Thong
@henryzw
youtube.com/henrythong
Page 64, 104, 160

Jessica Worland
jessicaworland.com
@jessicaworldstories
Page 186

Kati Douglas
xilophotography.com
@xilophotography
Page 198

For more stories—including a docuseries and podcast— visit **convertkit.com/stories**.

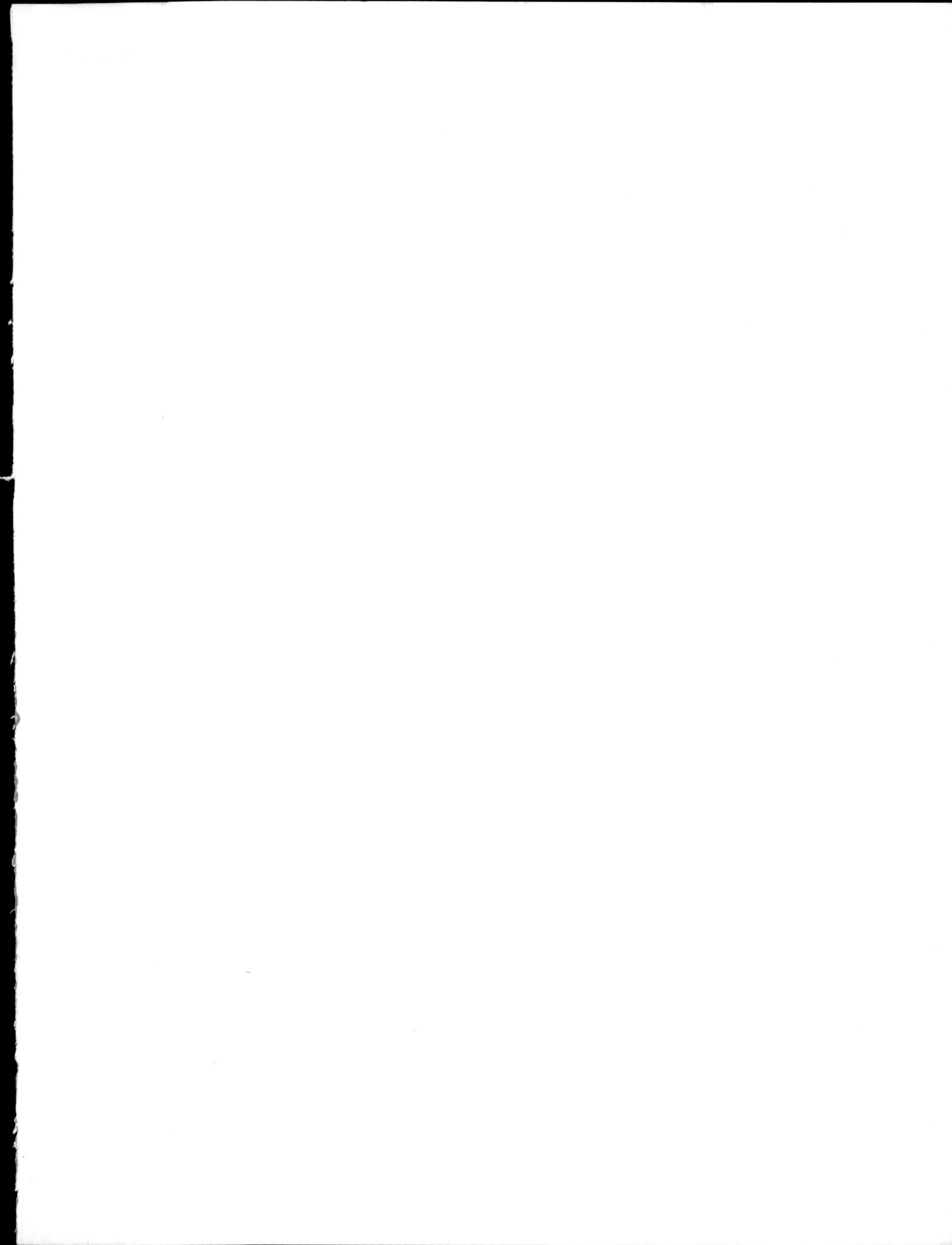